LOVE
OUT
LOUD

LOVE
OUT
LOUD

#LOL

"A [MILLENNIAL'S] GUIDE TO ENLIGHTMENT"

NICOLE GIBSON

DEDICATION

Humanity, every morning I wake and ask, *"How can I serve humanity today?"* My love for humanity is the strength that inspires faith through each storm, each moment of doubt and fear. This book is an expression of my love for every person, every sentient being, and specifically for *you*.

The Lovers and Messengers, those of you who choose to love unconditionally, in a world that reiterates its foolishness. Those of you who dedicate their lives to the upliftment of others, who choose adventure and courage over mediocrity.

My Team, how could this not be dedicated to you? All of the people that have stood by me through the ups and downs, my various moods, and the insufferable perfectionism. Thank you for continually believing in me and my dream. Let our light shine, and our vision be strong. Thank you for standing with love.

Jess, you showed me what true love is, how it feels, and how it transforms us. You activated and inspired my words; our love wrote this book. You showed me a vulnerability and a sensitivity that altered my world forever and tilted me on an axis. The love I have in my heart for who you are, where you've come from, and what you are for this world, is eternal. I hope our spirits continue to dance through the cosmos; because I know this is not the first time we've collided. I'm grateful for you everyday, and I know you will do amazing things in this life. I speak to you each time I look to the moon for guidance and the sun for strength.

CONTENT S

PREFACE

Falling in love is where it ends and begins. Its pivotal, and transformative in every sense of the word. Love is its own sense, yet entirely senseless. Love is not finding perfection, it's the unconditional permission to explore the imperfection. It's the free fall into infinite possibilities; the hazy, blurred, uncharted areas of one's heart, mind and soul. Love is the entry point into the deepest part of yourself. The portal to see beyond the physical reality and transcend into the land of magic. The space to revisit trauma and transmute it into something meaningful. It's the clarity at the end of an endless succession of events, leading you to now. It's the raw, messy and completely vulnerable chaos that helps tear us apart so that we can be remade in the face and image of love. Love is the earthquake that shakes the grounds of everything you think you are, to give you the profound opportunity to meet who you truly are.

Who you are is unbelievably lovable. I want you to know this. I want you to know what it feels like to be unapologetic; to understand what's on the other side of heartbreak and what lies beneath all your ideas. I want you to know the feeling of being overcome, of surrendering... I want you to know the feeling of safety that comes with being caught when you jump, and the comfort of being contained in so much love that the deepest healing becomes possible. I want you to experience a love that helps you realise how futile the mind can be in the face of love. A love that forces you to reflect on all the times you thought your way into a false sense of ecstasy. I want you to experience a love that forever changes you, sets a precedent, a rhythm, a standard for everything you pursue in life. A love that transcends boundaries, and time, and space. A love that is all-knowing, creative and makes diamonds from the pressures of your pain. A love that opens up the entire universe to you and allows you to scrape the sky with your fingertips.

I promise it's possible.

The more I walk the path of self-discovery, the more I see what the ultimate romance is. Our relationship with life. After all, we are born alone, and thus we will die alone. The only consistency we'll ever truly find is the way we are choosing to show up for life; this moment, our choice, and the guarantee that no matter what happens the sun and moon will continue to rise. If we can find stability and solace in this, our ideas about love start to open up.

Awakening to the life's impermanence has forced me to change my single-focused idea of what a love story actually is. My hope for you is that you recognise you have already found the 'one'- you are already in the process of writing your romance, and you will continue to do so. Life will never leave you until you leave life. Until death do us part. The challenge is not in finding your one, but the realisation you are it. We need to wait for nothing in order to experience the love we are searching for. This book is a journey in understanding how to connect to the love inside of you, and how to start loving out loud.

A C K N O   W L E D G E M E N T S

Nat, the only person who's loved me through every moment of messiness. My rock and my best friend; one of the truest loves of my life. The backbone of all my memories. Your understanding, perspective, creativity, and perfectly matched weirdness enriches my life every day. You're the first person I call and the person I'd follow through fire. Words won't ever do it justice, but thanks for being the ultimate partner in crime.

Kat Dawes, you believed in me and held a higher ground for me through immense pain and confusion. Your genius and multidimensional talent are one of a kind and completely unrepeatable. I hold the deepest honour for who you are and the way our journey (of nowness) will continue to unfold together. I am always here for you, eternally grateful for you, and a home for you. I love you.

Mum, here I write my first book. Finally making sense of all those lined pages sprawled across my bedroom as a teenager, finally being able to put the pieces of myself together, finally finding the clarity through the challenges. As I've put myself together, I found you. Who you were at my age, the free spirit with long brown hair, the lady leader that wouldn't be silenced, the trailblazer that blazed my trail. It's here I realise I am you, as you are me. It fills me with such a deep love. I see you, Mum, and although vulnerability is scary, and although some scars won't ever fade completely, those who see us will always hold us. I believe the loudest words of support are those found in another's silent actions. Please know how much I strive to make you proud. Thank you for all that you've taught me, and all that you are.

Dad, your commitment to giving me the best head start in life is something I've learned to become more and more grateful for each day. My education and exposure to travel and culture informs my views, and is woven into the change I make in the world, and the woman I am today. The commitment I have to my message, and the work I do each day, is highly connected to how much I want to make you proud, and do justice to the life you've provided for Matthew, Daniel and me. Your entrepreneurial spirit inspires me every day, Dad. I love you.

Annie, thank you for being a light through the storm, thank you for seeing me and seeing my heart. Thank you for reviving my love. Thank you for holding me and believing in me. Your beauty shines so brightly.

Sam, thank you for your ongoing support and commitment to this message, and to me. You have a remarkable amount of faith and tenacity. I honour the journey we have walked together.

Catherine, such a deep gratitude for your support through this writing and creation process. Your capacity to hold a container for a project of this nature is a testament to the depth of your love and understanding. Your guidance as my coach, and as a friend, has been invaluable. Thank you for being a partner in *love* as we bring this message to the world.

INTRODUCTION

In the past seven years, I have worked directly with 250,000 people as a speaker, a transformational facilitator, coach, and as CEO of The Rogue & Rouge Foundation. In this time, I've presented over 2,500 workshops and presentations, spending thousands of hours on stage. Due to the vulnerable and confronting nature of my speaking and facilitation style, I have been privileged to get to know the participants in my workshops. I have had a transformative journey in really, deeply, learning about human nature.

As a teenager, I secured my first major corporate sponsorship to travel Australia for 18 months delivering transformative workshops to remote communities, and shortly afterwards I became a finalist for The Young Australian of The Year 2014. That same year, I was given the Pride of Australia Medal, and The Financial Review, alongside Westpac, listed me as one of Australia's Top 100 Influential Women. I've had some radical opportunities and experiences. At 21 years old I was honoured to become the Commonwealth's youngest ever National Mental Health Commissioner, advising directly to the Health Minister and Prime Minister, whilst remaining CEO of The Rogue & Rouge Foundation, a mental health charity I founded at 18 after my own lived experience with anorexia nervosa.

I've had the privilege of being hosted by some of the world's most influential institutions, such as Oxford University, and spoken at some of the most prestigious international conferences. This has been an incredible juxtaposition from the thousands of young people and service providers I've worked with in extremely remote and rural areas across Australia, whilst trekking and adventuring through some of the furthest removed parts of the world to better understand culture, community and rites of passage.

My insatiable hunger to learn more about what our fundamental drivers are only ever increases the more I do the work I do. Through seeing the repeated patterns in our human needs and desires, irrespective of the context, I became convinced beyond any doubt that there is far more of what makes us the same, than what separates us. Our need for love and connection is universal and essential. We cannot thrive in states of disconnection, whether that's as an individual, a community, a workplace, or a nation.

My work has held a magnifying glass over some of the most significant gaps in our modern-day society. Our breakdown of intergenerational rites of passage has manifested as large and often debilitating fears of change, and an inability to cope with transitions in a healthy way. We maintain and encourage our young people's initiation into adulthood to centre around substances and peer-pressures, whilst a quarter of our elderly population is on antidepressants. Australia has one of the highest usages of antipsychotic and antidepressant medications globally, yet we're one of the most economically thriving and abundant countries in the world. So, what are we missing?

Some of the world's greatest minds have proven to us, again and again, our need for connectedness. Man's search for meaning has been a theme through every civilisation, every great leader, scientist, and philosopher. *We awaken to ourselves through each other.* We have an extremely fragile interdependence, and as our world becomes more and more self-focused, and the millennial generation are named "the selfie generation", it is becoming harder and harder to find our way back to the truth. We need to cut through the distraction and superficiality.

It's important that all of us are given a roadmap to understand the journey of self-love, so we know,, and accept, our need to love and to be loved. It's beyond me as to why and how this has not yet been incorporated into our education systems. Love has been the single most transformative energy in my life, both in how it's shaped and moulded my healing and my journey, as well as the transformative impact I've been able to have on hundreds of thousands of people. Sometimes people hesitate when they hear the word "love", and that's because of its deep confrontational nature. Love has the power to bring to light all of our shadows and to birth us into a new state of being. Now is the time for this to happen.

In 2020 mental illness is set to be the world's leading health epidemic and the biggest health epidemic in history to date. Suicide is now the leading cause of death in under 45's in Australia- more than car accidents, cancer and overdoses, taking the lives of eight Australians each day. We have half of Australians battling a mental illness at some point in their life.

More than ever we need to understand this is a symptom of a much deeper issue, a reflection of our cultural narrative. It's not a political issue. It's our issue, our responsibility, and our solution to find.

Battling my own mental illness, and repeatedly listening to doctors tell me that my struggle was due to a chemical imbalance, without ever enquiring into the cultural and environmental influences, shocks me more and more in hindsight. We need to take a look at ourselves, and the way we are showing up for each other each day. It was the moments in time where someone stopped to offer me their presence and unconditional love that became the most defining pinnacles of my healing journey.

At 14, I decided that I wanted to pursue theatre, leaving a mainstream schooling environment to spend my last three years of high school at an academy for creative industries. It was through performance that I found a true sense of love and connectedness. I deem it both the best and worst period in my life. I was immersed in the learning environment of my dreams, yet I found myself in a battle of comparison. It was a war that left me defeated and exhausted at the end of every day. There was always a void to focus on: *not pretty enough, not talented enough, not smart enough, not skinny enough, not innovative or creative enough*.

'Not skinny enough' became my hook into anorexia. In 18 months, the eating disorder had rapidly taken over the reins of my mind, body and spirit. My worldview went from one of conquering the world, to being entirely consumed by managing and portioning my 300 calories for the day. It ruined my friendships, my relationship with my boyfriend, my connection with my family, my education, and my art. Day by day, the voice of the eating disorder played into the vulnerability of perfectionism inside me; breaking me down and making me its slave. Piece by piece, all of my light turned to black. By the time of intervention at 16, I felt empty, lifeless and hopeless. I was crying out for help, yet rejecting it by the same hand.

The path into the darkness of a mental illness is a self-focused journey. It's incredibly love-less. It's difficult to discover love when you're in a state of self-affliction and self-orientation. Within that mindset and state of insecurity, you become prone to believing everyone, and everything relates back to you. You become paranoid about what others may be thinking about you and obsessed with the perception they hold of you. My days were spent completed fixated on my relationship with perfection and control- never on how I could offer something to others. I didn't believe it was possible to contribute anything of value at this point. It wasn't until I started to look beyond myself that recovery became possible.

When I commenced my therapy, I finally hit my threshold of pain. I was hurting myself and robbing myself of potential, time and resources. It was an act of self-sabotage. It was all an expression of my self-loathing; this loathing orchestrated by the voice in my head. Every inch of me wanted to blame those around me yet the more I blamed others, the harder recovery became. It was all my doing.

It was my school principal who finally offered me a space to lay it all down. He is still one of the most incredible leaders I've known to date. He was one of the only people during this time who had enough love for me to share a moment of intense presence. He wasn't afraid to challenge me and wasn't thrown off by the confrontational nature of the situation, or my physical appearance.

During the initial few weeks of my diagnosis, my principal called me into his office and shared a story of a past student who had struggled in the same ways I was struggling. He spoke of his regret for not intervening in a situation that then escalated to a crisis point. He assured me that he wouldn't let that happened again. I sat there frozen; wanting to cry and run at the same time. He looked at me, his gaze equal parts stern and yet with so much love, and I momentarily gave him eye contact.

"Nicole, do you know what my favourite thing to do is every day after school?"

I shook my head.

"My favourite thing to do and always has been my favourite thing to do, when I get home from work is to have a beer," he continued.

I looked up from the ground to hold his eye contact a little longer.

"I'll make you a deal," he paused so he could lock his sincerity into me. "I'm not going to have a single beer until you reach your weight target. I don't care if it takes three months, or three years, I want to show you an act of selflessness that will hopefully make you feel like you're not alone in this journey. I may not understand what it's like to be going through what you're going through, but I know what it means to suffer; to feel like no one understands, and I know what it means to be working towards something that feels impossible."

The few tears in my eyes turned to sobbing; a mixture of relief, gratitude and piercing pain flooded through me. With this flood of emotions came a sudden realisation that there was no getting out of this process. I didn't fully realise it at the time, but it was this moment that changed the trajectory of my perspective, and my life. Others' approach towards me had always centred around avoidance and uncomfortableness- no one had ever had the strength to lovingly confront me. The fact that he didn't shame me, or create a separation between he and I, showed me a type of love that was strong enough to withstand the discomfort of my disordered reality.

This moment irrevocably changed my idea of what true leadership was. It showed me the power of empathy and holding space for someone without opinion or judgment. This moment showed me what it meant to be with someone truly. As I took the painful steps towards my recovery, this moment stayed with me and inspired me profoundly. It was the first example I had of the power of love to transform.

Although I knew this, it wasn't until the end of 2015, spurred by a shattering heartbreak, that I really stopped to dig deeper into the gifts that pain can offer us, and the way it invites a deeper capacity to demonstrate and understand love. I began to deconstruct what a journey back to love truly meant, what it really took to rise from the ashes of pain to remember our true nature.

I learned that pain has a wild spirit. It's not meant to be tamed or numbed. It's meant to be felt, wholeheartedly, without hesitation. Genuinely feeling pain meant I was stepping back from all my masks and truly meeting the depths of my own love. Through that pain, in the middle of that pain, we truly meet ourselves. We deepen our capacity to love, to practice compassion, understanding and forgiveness.

This journey, however, requires elements of facilitation. Through the journey of discovering how to Love Out Loud and actualise the love inside of you, you will be guided through the confrontational and crucial questions necessary to connect with who you really are. This is how we change the world- through awakening ourselves. It is here we realise that we are not separate from each other.

Try to see this book as a journey; guiding you through a series of hard-hitting questions designed to help you deeply inquire into how you see yourself and life. Questions that follow a circular framework back to yourself, assisting a transformation to take place internally. I've always believed that the quality of our answers is equal to the quality of the questions we're asking.

There are nine concepts explored throughout this book. Each will bring you a step closer to discovering the love inside of you. This process is designed to bring you a deep sense of clarity; a roadmap and framework to measure your choices and direction against. This journey has not been designed to tell you what to think, but rather provoke you to answer some pivotal and defining questions about your own personal philosophy.

It is important to remember that while we seek love, love is the one always seeking us. Love sought you out in the moment of inspiration to reach for this book, or perhaps it was just coincidence... The special kind: coincide-ence. I'm very happy we have coincided.

PART ONE

NOTES BEFORE COMMENCING

This book is an invitation to explore yourself. It's not about me having your answers, but rather offering my perception, for you to draw your conclusions and connect your own dots.

Let your journey be yours.

In knowing this, there are some prerequisites I strongly encourage (if not, insist) that you organise and plan prior to our commencement of Chapter One.

1. Journaling

The greatest minds in the world journaled, from Albert Einstein to Picasso, to Steve Jobs and Richard Branson. Journaling is offering yourself a space to reflect and develop that relationship with yourself and is highly conducive to growth. One of my greatest teachers said to me when I was 15, "80% of learning is in the reflection." That has only become truer, the older I've gotten.

1. I suggest you use a journal specifically for this process, to use when recommended, but also when you feel inspired to write and reflect.

2. You'll be asked at times to answer specific questions throughout the book, and I encourage you to take the time to be really present with this process and elaborate as much as you can. The more awareness you bring into this, the greater the outcomes, and more profound impact you will experience in your life.

2. Stream of Consciousness

Sometimes our conscious minds get in our way, or we become blocked or stuck. There's an exercise that has really helped me process my thoughts, feelings and reflections when I haven't been able to be purposeful in my journaling process. It's called *stream of consciousness writing*. The process is to sit with your question, or maybe even a theme (for example, belief, honesty or acceptance), and continue to write exactly what comes into your mind for a certain length of time, e.g. one A4 page. Even if what comes to mind seems unrelated gibberish, keep writing until more thoughts come.

This practice helps silent the judgment of our rational minds and connects us more deeply into what's happening for us subconsciously.

1. I suggest you do this throughout the book when you're asked questions that you feel overwhelmed by or stuck on. Time yourself for roughly five minutes, and just write continuously.
2. I also recommend doing this on all of the topics before and after you finish reading each chapter to track how your perception and insights change throughout this process.

You must become the master of your own process.

3. Meditation and Self-Reflection

Mediation is not about clearing your mind; it's the process of learning to not judge your thoughts and feelings as they arise. The practice of non-judgement is crucial for you throughout your journey of learning to Love Out Loud. Taking the time to meditate and tune into what is arising for you throughout this process, deepens and strengthens the transformation taking place. If you find it easier to go for a walk on the beach, or a bike ride, rather than sitting in silence, it's about giving yourself the space to enquire, become curious, and integrate what you're experiencing. This journey requires a and reverent presence, instead of continuously giving into the distractions around you.

1. I recommend giving yourself at least twenty minutes a day, as you go through this journey, to be with yourself and love yourself enough to enquire to what wants to emerge and arise from you throughout this process.
2. Listen to your quieter feelings, your loud judgements, and try to see it all through the lens of love, holding it in a space of compassion.

I can't wait to embark on this journey with you.

What are you searching for?

It was June 2013, and I was in the middle of the Australian desert. I was 20 years old and on my first national speaking tour, Champions for Change, travelling to the most unlikely parts of my country with my teammates (there were four of us, two in each van) and my puppy, Byron. We had been driving an average of eight hours a day down the west coast of Australia. It's never a great idea to drive at night because Kangaroos jump in front of your car the same way mosquitoes buzz around light. We had consciously tried to make the next roadhouse by sunset, but this particular night it was inevitable that we'd either have to drive into the night or park and sleep on the side of the highway.

At 50 degrees Celsius, the heat was so intense that the tarmac looked like water, and walking from the gas pump to the counter of the roadhouse melted our plastic thongs. We'd often be greeted by strange characters. They weren't much the talking types; we were lucky to get a nod of acknowledgement. Two teenage girls from the city travelling these parts was a sight for sore eyes that's for sure.

On this particular afternoon, dusk was setting across the vast red cliffs in the distance. I had turned up the static radio station to break up the silence and the sound of the van's diesel engine in overdrive at 110 kilometres an hour. After a much needed sing along, I asked my teammate if she wanted to pull over to watch the sunset.

In silence, we sat on top of the 1970's Camper and looked out to the sun setting like a magnifying glass over the earth. It was nice to have a rest from the sound of the engine. Looking out as the sun inched closer to the horizon, I realised I couldn't even hear the cicadas. I'd never experienced a silence quite like it. I finally understood what people had meant when they used the term "deadly silent"- it felt like I was melting into the landscape. Captured by the desert sunset in front of me, I felt like God was painting, through my own eyes, the most incredible perfection I had ever seen. After ten or so minutes, I became aware I was in a deep trance-like state (a deep meditation). I looked down at the hairs on my arms and legs standing upright. My whole body was covered in goosebumps. Tears started to well in my eyes as I looked back to the sunset, which had almost left the horizon. By the time we saw the last glimpses of the sun, I was crying real tears. I realised this had been the first time I had cried in a long time. I was crying because I was so moved. Something in my soul was set on fire, as intensely as the sunset.

In that silence I found truth, and for the first time, I consciously realised it. I connected to who I was. Not through conversation, or explanation, but through silence. A piercing silence; becoming one with the beauty of Mother Earth. I was filled with a very memorable sense of nostalgia as I reflected on all the moments, and all the pain, that I had overcome to finally actualise my dream. I was set free. The sunset burnt holes through my doubt, insecurity and self-hate.

I had been funded to travel the country spreading a message of love to 50,000 young people. I was thousands of kilometres away from my identity, my comfort zone, and any limitation that had previously defined me. I had left a university degree (against the better judgement of family and friends) and gone from an aspiring actress; crippled by the pressures of perfection and other people's ideas of success, to having all of my worldly possessions in this one van. And, in this, I found peace; I found freedom. I realised that the belief in my soul was stronger than pride and doubt. I knew I was exactly where I was meant to be. I was initiated into the present moment; a place and space where all my trauma dissipated like grains of sand in the desert wind. I felt the most profound, most unconditional love for all things, myself included. Such a perfect love that no words can ever truly capture it in its entirety (but I will do my best in this book). My belief became so strong and I realised what I had been searching for. I understood that in order to live out our dreams and to let go of fear, we first must believe that it's possible. Belief is the first pillar to awakening. Believers are the pioneers of our awakening as a species.

And this leads me to ask you a question, just as I had to ask myself a series of questions before I finally found my answers.

What are you searching for?

Really. Not superficially, but really. So often we aren't honest with ourselves. It's much safer and more comfortable to say we want for less than what our heart desires. To say we want predictable things, easily attainable goals. It's harder to state what we want out loud. For what we want is the picture of what it is we truly love. It's a reflection of our deepest desires, what we truly value, and it can be overwhelming and frightening to entertain the idea that we're worthy enough of receiving it. The crazy thing is that we desire what we know, on some level, we're capable of attaining. It's the pathway of your heart. And the power of love is more than equipped to bridge the gap between your reality and your imagination.

As you start to awaken to the true nature of love, it may feel like Hagrid has finally come to tell you that Hogwarts is real. You may start to feel an overwhelming sense of magic as your paradigms open and possibilities you never thought of begin showing up. This is a natural result of expanding your perspective.

Before we go deeper in the journey, it's important to understand some principles of love. There's much misconception around what love is, and it's important to bust these myths.

(LOL) Love **OUT LOUD**

PRINCIPLES OF THE BOOK

1. Love is not found in another, it is a self-perpetuated experience.

2. Love is your nature.

3. Becoming complete with love is a process of aligning your heart and mind.

4. Life is not happening to you, you are happening to life; the outside world is a mirror of your internal world; to reach a state of self-love is to see love (you) in all things.

5. Evolution is happening, regardless of whether we consciously participate in it.

Really take your time with these points, they're crucial principles to understand this journey.

COINCIDE-ENCE NOT COINCIDENCE

We will often experience these new-found possibilities as synchronicity. I began to experience many of them in the months leading up to the tour. At first, the experience of coincide-ence was a lot to come to terms with - it felt like the world was moving around me.

In December 2012 as a nineteen-year-old, I was walking to my local shop when my mind started to race with all the recent synchronicities I had been experiencing. In that moment, I felt compelled to sit, and looking to my right, saw a vegetarian restaurant. The couches looked enticing, so I sat down and closed my eyes. In an attempt to quieten my racing thoughts, I decided to reach out to a higher power I wasn't quite sure I even believed in.

"Give me a sign, if this is all real, and I'm not actually losing my mind, please give me a sign."

As I opened my eyes, I saw this radiating man looking at me. Grinning at me, he called out,

"What makes you happy?"

I stumbled over my words, but eventually managed to ask, "Did you just read my mind?"

"I believe there's really only one. One mind, that is."

I was dumbfounded. "I was just asking for a sign."

He laughed and ate one of his kofta balls, "A sign for what?"

"I've been experiencing a lot of weird things lately and I've been having some weird dreams. Last night I had a dream that I bought a van and was travelling Australia speaking to teenagers."

He lit up, "I just got back from touring Australia!" He proceeded to explain that he was touring and spreading happiness through teaching drumming. He had the most beautiful spirit. I had never seen someone embody so much elation and joy.

I asked him if he believed in coincidences, and he replied, "No way!

Synchronicities are our spirit winking at us!"

"How do you know?" I asked.

He laughed, "All it takes is belief."

Believing is seeing.

He hugged me, said goodbye, and got into his van which was parked outside. I could see at least twenty drums through the back windows as he drove off. My smile was huge as I slumped back into the couch, shaking my head from side to side. I had been experiencing so many crazy encounters at the time, but this was the first time that I had really believed that we create our realities. I watched my own manifestation unfold within seconds, and from then on, I never looked back; I was a believer. Things happen for a reason.

Initially, it's common for synchronicities to be passed off as coincidences, yet the more you judge them, ignore them, or brush them off, the louder they become. This is because your consciousness is trying to guide you to a place of belief. When you start to believe that there is something incredibly powerful and infinite guiding you, you will start to bridge two worlds; the infinite with the finite. Belief is the first step in awakening. Until you believe that something more than what you can currently see is possible, you cannot create it. We learnt this as kids, right? Peter Pan taught it to us, yet as we grow up, we get told 'seeing is believing' when in actual fact 'believing is seeing.' Belief is a powerful force and marks the foundations of our experience of the world.

BELIEFS AND THE BRAIN

The brain is always seeking to prove itself right. That's how it works, no matter how bizarre, irrational or wonderful the things you tell it are. When you believe something, you are taking on something subjective (which everything always is) as fact, and this becomes a belief system through which you view the world. A basic example of this is we are told the sky is blue as children. This is then validated by those around us, and we accept this as a fact. Once this has been accepted as a fact, it then integrates itself into our psyche as a belief system; "I know the sky to be blue."

In the example of the sky, this may seem to have little or no negative effect on your experience of life. However, think about this in terms of other belief systems you may hold that could potentially, if left unexamined, diminish your ability to reach your potential. You are told as a child that you are not smart by your teacher. This is then reinforced by your classmates adopting that opinion, and mocking you for it. Because this is being validated by those around you, you take it on as a belief about yourself. This belief system then impacts the broader choices you make in your life like your high school subjects, university entry, and the choice of your career.

Often the beliefs we hold about ourselves have no rational justification, but are in fact a result of adopting other people's opinions of us without taking on a deeper sense of enquiry. We do much of this belief-making as children, before our ability to analyse situations rationally has fully developed.

Just before my diagnosis of anorexia nervosa, the tension between my parents and I was like a thick blanket suffocating me anytime I was in the same room as either of them. I have extremely vivid and distinct memories of this time in my life.

My deeply ingrained belief system of unworthiness was the key driver in pushing myself to anorexia's limits.

One evening I had refused to come to the dinner table. I was so exhausted. I was half unconscious in my bed when my Mum asked my Dad to force me to come and eat dinner with them. I could feel the ache and crippling pain in my body even at the thought of moving from my bed. The reality that my doctor had highlighted to me was that I had the bone density of someone double my age; this had started to feel very real, and my helplessness was growing. My parents struggled to understand or empathise with me during this time, because after all, this was all self-inflicted. This often meant their approach with me was harsh and aggressive; communicating their frustrations abrasively.

I dragged myself to the dinner table, mentally preparing myself for yet another night of eating in silence. The sound of knives, forks, and chewing ripped shreds through me. I was doing everything in my power to not freak out. To explain this level of sensitivity to someone who doesn't understand is one of the most debilitating feelings that exists.

After thirty minutes, having finished their own meals, they sat there watching me. I hadn't made much progress, and I asked if I could go to the bathroom. I felt like a prisoner in my own home. In reality, I was shackled to the voice in my own mind telling me how pathetic I was.

They couldn't say no to my request, so I went to the en-suite in my bedroom and stood staring at myself in the mirror. I could feel my heart racing with the same amount of adrenaline a marathon runner would have. I had a choice between the voice of my parents, and the voice of my eating disorder. Looking at my bloodshot eyes in the mirror, I had the voice of anorexia yelling at me to get rid of everything in my stomach. Then, in opposition, was the stress of my parents hearing, or potentially catching me out. It was like trying to choose which type of torture is preferable.

The thing about mental illness is that there's no escape from your own mind. Without the ability to un-invest in these thoughts, they define your whole experience of reality. In this moment, and thousands of similar moments, anorexia had convinced me that it wasn't just my dinner on the line, it was the entirety of my self-worth. It was the difference between another three days of self-punishment or having a sense of relief and peace of mind so that I could sleep that night. Yet, because this was an invisible war, no one could understand. Least of all my parents.

The anxiety I felt returning to the dinner table was immense, having thrown up the contents of my dinner. I put my head down and felt the weight of my parent's gaze on me. I was silently praying for them to not ask the question. Under the safety of the table, my hands and legs shook with terror. This terror compounded with the prospect of having to lie to them yet another time; simply because I had no way of explaining the reality inside my head and broke down in front of them. Watching me, they asked me if I had thrown up dinner. I cried and yelled and pleaded with them that I hadn't. The reality was that this dramatic display of dishonesty was just a means for me to convince myself, regardless of all logic, that I was still in control.

It's been a journey to feel worthy enough to heal and be healthy. It's been a journey to believe I'm worthy of meaningful relationships with my loved ones and myself. It's been a journey to believe I can be loveable, even when I'm imperfect, and to realise that true love is holding someone in their imperfection. The reason I struggled so much with honesty, was because I couldn't overcome my fears rooted in perfectionism. I wanted to edit myself in a way that meant other's never saw my vulnerabilities and struggles. There was no way I could heal until I looked at how I could change my belief systems.

BELIEFS ARE FILTERS WE SEE THE WORLD THROUGH

Before we become conscious of the nature of belief systems and how they act as filters, it's very confrontational and often triggering to have our belief systems challenged. When our belief systems are challenged, we enter a state called cognitive dissonance (the state of having inconsistent thoughts, beliefs or attitudes, especially relating to behavioural decisions and attitude change). We experience this when we are confronted with something that is either challenging something we believe or is directly showing us our belief system may not be real.

In this state, we have two options:

1. **To accept what's in front of us, and alter our belief.**

2. **To reject what's in front of us, and hold on to our belief.**

For the most part, humans are incredibly stubborn and will choose the former, because to accept and change our belief system means to swallow our pride and become teachable. If you want to grow, it's essential to become teachable. At the most vulnerable time of my eating disorder, I had to open my mind and become teachable. I had to admit there were things I didn't know; to allow my perspective and belief to grow into something new and more nurturing for me. As soon as we believe we know all there is to know, we separate ourselves from everything, and everyone, putting our own evolution on hold. Being teachable requires a great deal of humility and a constant practice of managing our egos. The brilliant thing about knowing that we have the ability to change our belief systems is knowing that we have the freedom and capability to choose belief systems that serve us. We can then create a relationship of friendship and cheerleader with our brains, rather than that of an enemy who is continually justifying our comfort zone and, therefore, preventing us from moving forward in life.

WHY IS THE BRAIN WIRED LIKE THIS?

The brain is the calculator for your heart. It's a computer system designed to help you get what you want and to keep you alive. The most primitive form of the human brain, the 'reptile brain', has been evolving for two million years. The reptile brain is fuelled by reactionary triggers that help us make rapid choices (known as fight, flight or freeze)- useful for when we were surrounded by primal threats and needed to survive in the wilderness.

As we became more sophisticated, we began to develop the monkey brain (which helps us with resourcefulness, and building equipment/ tools), before finally developing our prefrontal cortex (which allows us to make conscious, rational choices that help us evolve and learn at a more rapid rate). In understanding this, you can begin to learn how to control the mind and operate from the prefrontal cortex more consistently.

THE BRAIN IS WIRED FOR SURVIVAL, NOT HAPPINESS

Most of us have not been trained to listen to our impulses and instincts. When we hesitate during decision-making it sends stress triggers to the back of our brain. We all have a remarkable internal guidance system that is trying to communicate with us. I'm a big believer that our instincts and feelings know the direction we should be travelling. When we're not used to listening to our gut feeling, we develop a habit of hesitation. Our brain reads hesitation as a threat and rapidly looks for all the potential risks in the decision we're making and the surrounding environment. Often these 'risks' can be highly irrational (often a symptom of anxiety). These stress signals are also sending massive amounts of adrenaline through the body to help us make rapid and reactive choices. As a result, once we hesitate, it's then significantly harder to act. A really simple example would be going to ask for someone's number across the bar or speaking up in a meeting when you have something to say. We tend to be our worst enemies much of the time in these situations, hesitating and then buying into our doubts and fears. In these situations, we experience an initial impulse that is trying to spur you towards action, to beat your primitive brain. This impulse is your instinct. Once you hesitate and wait longer than a few seconds after your initial impulse, the brain will start registering the situation as a threat and calculating reasons you shouldn't act and should instead stay within your comfort zone.

We need to become masters of our own minds. The beginning step to this is understanding the way our neurology is wired. In re-training myself to think differently about myself and my life, I learnt that the brain relied heavily on repetition in order to learn something. Repetition is what strengthens neural pathways.

THE BRAIN LOVES REPETITION

We learn through repeated action. We master something by doing it so many times that it becomes automatic, like cleaning your teeth or driving a car. We form habits and rituals so they become easy. This is also true when it comes to how we talk to ourselves. When we are exposed to a certain way of thinking for long enough, these ways of thinking become our default. Our belief systems are thoughts we have about ourselves that we have rethought and reinforced continuously. The joy in understanding this is in the realisation that we are programmable. We have the power to deprogram ourselves and then reprogram ourselves to be attuned to positive self-talk. Negativity is often cultural - it has become a social norm that we don't question. It's much rarer to see someone who is secure, positive and confident within themselves than it is to see the opposite; someone battling insecurity and self-doubt. Our behaviours are conditioned, and only when we understand that this is a choice can we regain our free will and control.

If at first you feel that changing your self-talk isn't working, keep at your practice.

It takes roughly twelve weeks to reprogram a behavioural pattern. If you set yourself the challenge to catch yourself every time you say something negative about yourself, and actively reframe it, after twelve or so weeks this positive reinforcement will start to become a default. You will eventually reach a point of fluency.

Cognitive Behavioural Therapy Worksheet

Where were you?	What emotion or feeling were you experiencing?	Negative emotional thought.	Evidence that supports the thought.	Evidence that does not support the thought.	What is an alternative thought?	New feeling or emotion.

Here is an example of a Cognitive Behavioural Therapy graph that assists you in logging your thoughts so that you can become more mindful and conscious of how you speak to yourself.

When I began this practice, my self-talk was highly distressing. In fact, I never thought it would be possible to alter the way I talked to myself. As I stayed consistent in my journey, it ,sure enough, became a habit to speak positively to myself and put things into a solution-focused frame. It took commitment, but as my thoughts began changing, so did my reality. My belief systems altered and my quality of life drastically improved. It is a shortcut that allows you to live from a higher perspective at all times and normalises a compassion-based practice in your life.

THERE'S A SHORTCUT TO BUILDING EMPOWERING BELIEF SYSTEMS

LOVE.

Aligning yourself to love and compassion opens the mind, connecting it to an infinitely broad perspective. In life, we often hear that time is the only healer of our pain, when in actual fact it is what time brings that heals our pain.

With TIME comes PERSPECTIVE.

Perspective is the healer, and with perspective comes the ability to alter our belief systems about a situation. For example, you're experiencing a heartbreak, and due to the immediate circumstances, you may be telling yourself things like:

· "I will never feel better."
· "I will never find another person I love as deeply."

As time goes on, and the space that was once filled by the relationship is filled with new people and experiences, you begin to shift your view, and thus your beliefs around the experience of the relationship. As you open to other opportunities your heart begins to heal. This is because with new experiences, comes a broader perspective.

Now here is the shortcut. Love provides this bird's eye view of life at all times. When in a state of love, you're able to view things from a space of compassion, understanding, forgiveness, non-attachment, and infinite possibilities. This does not mean there isn't an important process that must be moved through- there is no shortcut to feeling your feelings. What an alignment to love does provide is a focal point during periods of heartache and adversity, which allows you to move in a single direction, towards healing; without the doubt that you're making the wrong choices for yourself, or digressing.

I've always believed that questions are the single most powerful instigator of expansion, transformation and direction. The quality of your life is largely influenced by the questions you are asking. One thing that I always remind myself, especially in regard to love, is:

1. Every question has an answer, and every problem has a solution.

2. Love is whole. Love is complete.

Adopting this mindset and incorporating these two premises into your life philosophy allows you to structure your belief systems and approach to life with forward motion. To believe all questions have answers, and all problems have a solution, keeps your awareness on solutions rather than on complications and problems.

If up until now you've been trapped in limited belief systems, know that there's been a perfection to your unfolding. Without the experience of being trapped in limitation, we can't understand the gifts in elation and liberation.

Our relationship to others and to the world has ultimately been the influences that have shaped our belief systems. Until we realise that we have the control over how we perceive this, it's difficult to master our minds and alter our harmful belief system.

WE EXIST ONLY IN RELATIONSHIP TO OTHER THINGS

Just as black has white, the day has night, and the southern hemisphere has the northern hemisphere, we live in relationship to things. We are in a relationship with all things. We exist in relationship to each other. For example, I discover myself in the way I relate to you. We also exist in relationship to our environments, circumstances and experiences. We have the ability to create the meaning of these relationships and the way we relate to them. It is through understanding and experiencing what we are not that we can truly understand what we are. Through the denial of love, through disbelief, we are then offered the insight into what love truly is. Often when we deny our true nature (love), we will experience pain and a lack of alignment. In many cases, it is only through reaching a threshold of unbearable pain that we will become inspired to commence a journey of understanding our true nature and transcending our limited circumstances.

To experience things separately allows us to be more whole with that singular experience, and to more deeply learn from it and understand it. Although the truth is that heads and tails are both parts of the same coin, we can only ever look at each side singularly at any one time. Buddhists call this The Law of Focus- you can only ever think of one thing at once.

Awakening to the fact I could *choose my beliefs*, choose what it was I was focusing on, revolutionised my experience of life. It still blows me away when an audience member visibly has an epiphany when I state the simple fact that *"we choose what it is we tell ourselves."* The reality that we have, or can develop, conscious control over our self-talk is still widely unknown. Yet, this is the precursor for any significant change to take place.

This really struck me when I was facilitating a workshop in the Western Australian Desert when afterwards, a young girl (15) wrote to me saying:

"I'm not sure how to start this but I'll just start with saying thank you. Today was the first day where I realized that I can consciously control my thinking and isn't that a crazy thought? Seeing you as a living, breathing example of someone who went out and accomplished dreams that were deemed 'unrealistic' is truly refreshing. Your talk was so riveting I did a little dance after - I am this able-bodied human with so much potential! I have limbs! And a brain! And I am aware! And I can do things with these limbs and this brain and actually accomplish things and change self-sabotaging thinking. I was so inspired and moved as if something actually dislodged itself inside me, and that is a sacred, sacred feeling - to think I can really be the best version of myself is a little scary but motivating. I used to think that following an unattainable dream was for hedonists who would have crazy highs but be stuck in lows - but your talk changed my view completely. I now think that dreams and aspirations are all we really have at the end of the day, it binds us together and makes us kinda human. I'd just like to say thank you, what you did and are doing is super inspiring, you're a great human being!"

Having heard of her struggles earlier that day in the workshop, I read her message in awe. She has been perpetually dismissed by others in her life who she had tried to reach out to. How could something so simple have had such a profound impact on someone's whole frame of thinking, and thus their life?

Knowing that we can alter our beliefs is the first powerful step toward transformation. Now that you know this, hold onto the belief that somewhere deep inside of you, you hold the answers to all of the questions you will be asked throughout this book.

I invite you to take some time to be present with the following questions. Write and reflect the answers in your journal, really trying to answer them in full, this is an important foundational awareness to take with you throughout the rest of this journey.

1. *Why have you arrived at this book? What are you searching for?*

2. *What are your negative belief systems?*

3. *What do you wish to believe about yourself?*

CHAPTER 2: HONESTY

What do you really want?

This is an intense question... what rises up in you when you read it?

What a strength there is in letting go of fear and fiercely stating what you want; in standing for your truth. There are very clear reasons as to why we struggle to access this confidence. Let's explore them:

NECESSITIES OVER NICETIES

It's an unfortunate cultural narrative that so many of us put niceties before necessities. The trap of being polite and modest prevents us from stepping into our truth. If you want to experience your power and your potential, honesty is a necessity.

This is something I have experienced many, many times. Honesty is a lesson that life has tested me on in very confrontational ways- particularly with my eating disorder. Secrecy became my normal. If I was to deconstruct why that was, it was a direct reflection on my lack of self-love. I wasn't being honest with myself, thus I couldn't be honest with other people. I was defending something that was hurting me, and rejecting those who loved me. I was in denial and believed I was completely in control of my addiction when the addiction had deep claws of control in me. Growing up lying about the simplest of things, like what you've eaten, creates deep subconscious programs around transparency and honesty, which I unconsciously carried into many of my relationships.

Dishonesty became habitual for me. It became a learnt, automatic behaviour, even down to the simplest of things. Most days I'd come home from school and I'd be fixated on getting to my room as fast as I could. It was a mixture of genuine exhaustion (needing to sleep), coupled with the deep desire to avoid the question, "What did you eat today?".

On the days I didn't manage to avoid the question, I would answer with a list of foods I knew would be acceptable to my parents, whilst doing my best to not give eye contact and avoid any further interrogation. At the time I felt no guilt. The force that was driving me was fear, and when you're in a state of fear *(a survival state)*, there's no room for connection, love, or truth.

Fear is ultimately what drives dishonesty.

Fear activates survival. In this state, we see others as a threat rather than a support. In this deep state of fear, I couldn't fathom the idea that another person could possibly have my best interests at heart. I didn't feel worthy of love.

So many of us feel that when someone lies to us, it's personal when in reality, it's merely a projection of their own fear. It's important to have compassion and to have the understanding that when we feel safe, we are able to have our guards down, be transparent and vulnerable. During the years of my eating disorder, I rarely felt safe (how could I when my demon was in my own mind), and this translated into behaviours of constant self-preservation. I couldn't see that by holding back my truth and being transparent about my needs, I was preventing myself from healing. Without placing all your cards on the table, you cannot make a plan to progress forward. You remain in a closed state, protecting yourself rather than expressing yourself.

We cannot heal what we don't reveal.

It really is true what they say; the truth will set you free *(but it's going to hurt like a bitch first)*. The truth, at times in my journey, has felt like a laser beam. Truth can be extremely intense, and often evoking deep feelings of denial, judgment and fear of rejection, before we finally accept it, in order to move forward. When we stand with truth, we become so much more powerful and liberated.

There's an immense gift in the initial discomfort that truth can create for us, and also the discomfort our truth can provoke in others. It propels us towards growth. Honesty is sometimes not nice; truth brings confrontation and sometimes pain. Truth has the power to break down our walls, our delusions, and grow us into more and more of ourselves. Of course, this is often an uncomfortable experience.

Love and **honesty** are one and the same. **Only with honesty can true alignment to love be experienced.**

Often, we've been taught that keeping the peace is more important than speaking our truth and that behaviour carries through to the way we speak to ourselves. This is rooted in the fear that our truth won't be accepted, or it will be too much for others to handle. So, we get trapped in reason and justification. It's important to remember that truth doesn't need to be justified, the truth simply always *is*. It has nothing to prove. As soon as you begin justifying an action or situation, you are speaking from rationality, not your heart.

The problem with holding back our truth for the sake of others' comfort, is that it holds us in a place where we cannot experience true intimacy or love. It is a barricade to true connection. It blocks vulnerability. When we stand in our truth and express honestly, we can in turn experience connection.

The only way through shame is to bring it to light.

Life has given me intense and confrontational experiences of facing the truth, which have been extremely important, defining moments in my personal growth and spiritual development. I feel in life we have gentler options to confront our truth before it comes to slap us in the face. For me, there have been several iterations of my life where I've avoided and denied the truth until it came crashing down on me.

This was particularly true during 2016 when I took a four-month soul searching trip around the world. In the final month of my journey, I completed a ten-day hike in Peru, sleeping in minus ten degree temperatures, at an altitude of 15,000 feet. I was tested on every level. The feelings of exhaustion and the intensity of the noise in my head pushed me to new levels of vulnerability as I reached the campground at the end of every day. I had spent a lot of my time in the mountains thinking and reflecting on my life back in Australia. The past three years had gone quickly, and I found my mind reverting back to the years I had spent in the van three years earlier. After I finished the hike, I travelled to the Amazon jungle where I spent five days in deep silence. To sit with myself in the most isolation I had ever experienced was painfully confronting. By day three I was brought to my knees as the thoughts became louder and louder in my head. The lessons of truth had revealed themselves to me once again, yet this time with more subtlety and intricacy. The demons of denial and suppressing my deeper knowing were demons I knew well, yet regardless of our familiarity, it never became easier to confront.

Amongst the raw nature of the Amazon, I thought I had hit a point of insanity. In truth, I was hitting my breaking point. An existential crisis. I went to the edges of my mind, the places where I had danced once before. The border of my belief systems. The dark dimensions where my demons lingered. The place where I could see beyond my identity and limited ideas about myself and the world. It's easier to ignore your demons when you're distracted. Here, in the Amazon, there was nothing but hard truths.

Silence is one of the key reasons I've been liberated.

Through experiencing solitude and silence, I've been able to access deep feelings of love and connectedness. It's very necessary that we all learn to be alone. We avoid the aloneness, and the silence, because it can bring to the surface our fears as well as quieter, more dormant feelings. Without a single distraction, I had to sit with my deeper feelings and the knowing inside my heart that I wasn't being congruent in my life. I had been ignoring myself, justifying my actions and believing my own lies.

I had left my relationship in Australia to travel for three months. I didn't make this decision selfishly- it was survival in many ways; I hadn't been in a good space back home. I had felt lost from myself, my integrity, and my own sense of sanity. I was madly in love, with no ability to stabilize the relationship. It was as if we held a mirror up to each other, highlighting the darkest corners of each other's past. I had felt alienated from my friendships and professional relationships. My world had started to feel incredibly polarised.

During this time, I had been spending most of my weekdays in other cities or communities, working with hundreds of people; the compliments brushing over the empty spaces inside of me, never sticking. Something in me at this point in my life was incapable of receiving acknowledgement and love. I felt like a failure. Riddled with guilt, shame, and anxiety, I'd return to my partner most weekends and the feelings of polarisation where often difficult to reconcile and integrate. We didn't know how to reconnect in a healthy way which often led to weekends fuelled by substances. Escaping the sobering reality of our love, I became incredibly dependant on this escape- often finding myself in hotel rooms during the week fantasizing about the feelings of connectedness we'd emulated in the late hours of the night under the influence. The nagging voice in my mind that knew this escape took me far away from the leader I wanted to be, would be silenced by the aching in my heart to feel a sense of comfort. It was a painful dichotomy.

I was in the midst of grappling with a different kind of addiction. I was addicted to our love, the dysfunction, and the feeling of going to sleep at sunrise next to her. Yet, once again, I was in complete denial. The demons of dishonesty had crept back and wrapped their vines around me.

She needed me there, yet was so quick to push me away that I spent much of my energy trying to re-centre myself; bringing myself back from emotional edges. I'd never felt rage or uncertainty like I did with her. Through the relationship, I was forced to meet the violence and aggression inside myself. It helped me realise that this expression of anger *is love getting lost in translation* much of the time. Perhaps that's all that hate ever is.

I would spend most days feeling unheard, having my heart yearn so deeply for understanding. Many times in the relationship I'd think back to my upbringing, how my parents would resort to aggression to try and get me to listen. I was repeating the patterns I had resented so much. This is true for all aspects of our life; we will continue to repeat patterns and play various roles until we have resolution with our wounds until our wounds fade to faint scars through the power of love.

It was in the Amazon that I had to feel the reality of how disassociated I was. It felt like all the fragments of me that I'd thrown far off into the universe, were crashing down on me, all at once. It felt like this incredible pressure in my mind, on my shoulders, and all through my chest. This was the feeling of truth reaching out to me again and reminding me to come back to my path.

When we listen to the quieter feelings inside, it can feel extremely painful. If we listen close enough, we can feel the distance between our minds and hearts. The greater the pain, the more significant the neglect has been. The longer we ignore ourselves, the harder it is to feel our way back into alignment. Remember in these times that the pain is just your distance of growth, and to realign yourself to truth is to always move in the right direction. It hurts far less to feel the pain momentarily, then to experience a lifetime of dishonesty and regret. I learnt this the hard way after years and years of deeply ingrained secrecy developed through my illness. It was an extremely difficult lesson to learn, and a hard behaviour to change, yet the commitment to working through these challenges has gifted me a continually flourishing life, with such a breadth of connection and experiences.

The decision to be more honest with ourselves, and others, requires the ability to communicate honestly. Communication is a core component to being able to live in your truth. Though it may be difficult at first, honest communication becomes much easier when these three statements are vocalised in relationships with others, and to ourselves.

1. I WANT

2. I NEED

3. I FEEL

Often, when we don't understand how to take responsibility for our own thoughts, emotions and perception of an experience, we tend to project onto others. By this, we blame others for how we're feeling and blame them for not being able to meet our needs to 'fix' how we're feeling. When we project, we attack others. When someone is feeling attacked, the normal response is to defend. In this state of attack and defence, there is no space for conversation or resolution. It becomes a merry-go-round, often leaving all parties unfulfilled and drained. In order to resolve conflict, we need to be able to state our own position, without blame or attack, and allow others to do the same. If this happens, there's then the capacity and space to both feel heard, acknowledged and negotiate the best way forward.

What are the barriers stopping us from confidently stating our wants, needs and feelings? I've noticed some key themes from facilitating workshops with 250,000 people.

1. People are afraid to vocalise what they want, need, or feel, out of fear that they will change their minds.

2. People are afraid of the prospective outcomes from voicing the truth; for example, someone else's rejection or judgment of them.

3. People aren't in tune with their wants, needs and feelings, and can't place them.

The risk in not knowing these is we are then susceptible to external influences. We become disconnected from our own internal guidance system, and risk being led astray.

Often when people come to me for coaching, guidance or facilitation, I notice similar stories in their pain. They are disconnected from themselves. Their relationship with themselves is either non-existent, or has been fractured, abandoned or neglected. They have prioritised others at the expense of themselves, and often this is because they have been unable to communicate what their wants, needs and feelings are.

A recent client came to me feeling challenged. She had been working for her family business, and due to her family's connection to their culture, one of her main values was to honour and support her family. She was stressed, unsettled and often unable to place the way she felt about particular elements of her situation. She knew that she felt voiceless and as though her needs and wants weren't being met.

When we broke it down, she had a strong need for creative expression, personal and professional growth, and independence. She wanted a working environment that was separate from her personal world. She felt guilty, frustrated, trapped, and static (unable to progress forward in her life). Once we had mapped her wants, needs and feelings, we drew up the reality of her situation in the family business. Here it became clearer (in an objective sense), whether or not the family business had the capacity to support her into a space of deeper fulfilment. It also created a map of communication, meaning she was clearer around what the challenge was actually rooted in, which meant she could approach her family with more objectivity, rather than a constant back and forth of attack and defence. This often happens when the individuals involved in the situation are unable to take responsibility for their own wants, needs and feelings.

Clarity is crucial for resolution. Becoming more and more honest with yourself and others will immediately land you in a space of deeper clarity.

It's important to understand that truth is the state that honesty creates. Through a practice of honesty, we move closer and closer to our truth.

I see it like this:

TRUTH IS A STATE OF BEING

Truth: [the state or quality of being true]: that which is true or in accordance with fact or reality: tell me the truth | she found out the truth about him.

HONESTY IS THE PRACTICE

Honesty: [the quality of being honest]: to be aligned with the truth: the word "honest" originates from a Latin word 'honestas' which means 'honour and respectability) - to honour someone (a verb).

When honesty becomes your practice, truth will be your outcome.

TRUTH AND VULNERABILITY

Truth is automatically vulnerable, however, the truth is that vulnerability is an incredible strength, because truth is an armour that coats us in our vulnerability.

We spend so much time running away from truth because of the way it exposes us. Standing in our truth strips us naked. We enter a space of deep vulnerability. There's no defence and no pretence. We're completely open. As society evolves we're beginning to look at vulnerability through a different lens; seeing it as a source of strength- which I fundamentally agree with. However, it's important to understand what the word vulnerability actually means. It comes from the Latin word vulnerare, which translates directly as wound, or 'to wound.' The word is anchored in pain. This is because when we are vulnerable, our wounds are exposed and we become susceptible to getting hurt. Vulnerability is the practice of being able to expose yourself, irrespective of the risk, and back yourself completely. There's so much power in this practice. It requires a deep, deep level of honesty with yourself and complete self-acceptance. It requires loving yourself enough to be unaffected by others potential attempts to bring you down. True strength is being impenetrable, irrespective of attack, because you do not need others' approval or validation.

If you lie to someone in order to 'get ahead', you are then exposed to the possibility of being caught, and therefore attacked- and not in a way which cultivates strength. If you willingly expose your truth, you can be secure in knowing that there is nothing to fault or question in what you're exposing.

You have access to immediate clarity around who has enough love to accept your true self, and who does not. When you put truth on the line, and expose yourself, you open yourself to potential judgment; however, it becomes very clear in these situations, that this is a reflection of the other person's bias or judgement.

As William Shakespeare so eloquently said; *"No legacy is so rich as honesty."*

In many ways, we've been told that hiding our feelings is the only way to protect ourselves. We've been taught that closing down is less painful than opening up and that running away is freedom. We've been taught that blaming someone else shifts the responsibility. Relating this back to the story of my client, the repeated pattern of the situation was the constant blame she would project onto her family. The reality of the situation was that she was unfulfilled and not taking responsibility for communicating this. Instead, she was blaming her family for unrelated problems, in turn creating further conflict without the space for resolution.

TAKING RESPONSIBILITY

The truth cannot be fucked with. Nor can we when we take full responsibility for ourselves.

To be fully responsible for yourself is to always be empowered. To be fully responsible for yourself is to always see love reflected back to you, in whatever form it shows up. This is no one else's responsibility.

1. You are responsible for your happiness.

2. You are responsible for your experience of love.

3. You are the reason you experience love.

If you deflect responsibility, then you are left as a victim of your circumstances; this is commonly seen in our social narratives with each other, and even in mainstream therapies. If a perpetrator of any kind has hurt you, and you were innocent in the situation, of course, it seems that you're the victim of your circumstances. As soon as you claim your experiences as yours, as soon as you own your story, which means taking responsibility for yourself and your life, you have the opportunity to step into your power and control the levers of your destiny.

RESPONSIBILITY IS THE ABILITY TO RESPOND

In all moments, we have the ability to respond to our circumstances. The more we learn to regulate ourselves, the more we will be able to respond to life, rather than react to it. When we react to life we become powerless, losing our control. This is true even in instances of pain. The stronger and more practised we become, the more we are able to consciously create our futures from our experiences, and not be a victim of our pasts.

Part of taking responsibility is to understand the nature of blame. One of the life hacks that has fundamentally changed the way I communicate is the understanding that inside blame is the awareness of a need. When we can identify this, we go from blaming others to being able to take responsibility for what our needs are, and then communicate and navigate our circumstances and relationships more consciously.

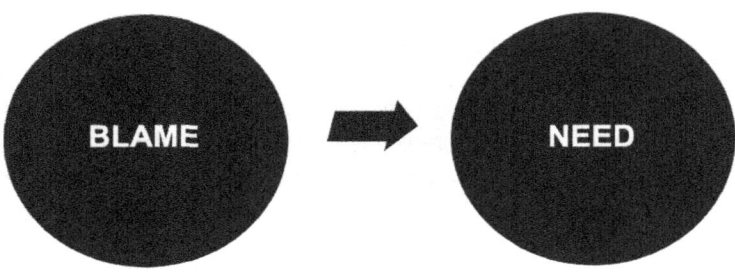

For example; "You're never here from me" (blame) translates as; "I need you to be here for me more" (need). When we communicate our needs, we create a space of clarity and open communication. When we blame, we often receive defence or withdrawal.

It can sometimes be difficult to understand what the need under the blame truly looks like when so few of us have had it role modelled. It's rare to come across a person who has reached total acceptance of who they are and lives in all moments as the fullest expression of themselves. Many of our role models, whether they're politicians, authority figures or celebrities, are tangled up within their own fears. Not until we find those role models who are completely authentic, do we see our possibility mirrored back at us. There are great people who have walked this planet and demonstrated this. Truth tellers. Truth seekers. Those who truly, wholeheartedly dedicated themselves to loving out loud.

REFLECTIVE CHALLENGE

Reflect on the last three times you blamed someone. Also note what sort of dynamic was created as a result of blaming instead of taking responsibility for your own feelings and needs. It's important to understand that when we blame others, we immediately go into a state of attack, which means our counterpart will automatically go into a state of defence. In this dynamic, we can't find the middle way, and it becomes impossible to reconcile situations. More importantly, we will often leave feeling unheard. This is because what it is you actually needed was never communicated.

As you reflect on the last three times you resorted to blame in various circumstances, identify what your needs were in those situations.

1.
2.
3.

Now, I want you to think of the past three times someone else blamed you for something. What might their needs have been in those situations? This is a great tool to deepen your understanding and compassion for others.

1.
2.
3.

Truth is the highest frequency we can access; it's complete alignment and something to embrace. A friend once told me: "Truth is an armour. My Dad told me that he would love me no matter what, and would always protect me, but if I lied... he couldn't protect me because he wouldn't know who he was protecting."

You are loved. But if you refuse to be you, how can you draw love into your life? The insecurity and self-hate will fade away when you embrace all that you are, without judgement. The magic is when you stand strong in yourself, and start to be love, through action and demonstration, instead of fighting for it, or striving for it. Simply be it.

Standing in truth, and being honest with yourself about what you want, will move you into a state of deeper flow. You will begin to experience more ease and less resistance.

IDENTIFYING WHAT YOU TRULY WANT

In the process of identifying what it is you actually want, you will be confronted by the parts of yourself that don't believe having what you want is truly possible. These are your perceived limitations. As discussed in Chapter One, believing something is possible is the first step to being able to create it.

Desire is the easiest way to identify what it is you truly want. What are you drawn to? Desire often has shame or guilt associated with it. It's an unacknowledged part of our broader cultural narrative. It's less important to dive into how that came to be, and more important to explore and address this reality.

When I first left school and started my university degree, it became apparent to me that my desires extended far beyond the predetermined pathways laid out by our education systems. I would sit in my marketing lectures, the sound of my lecturer's voice drowned-out by my inner-monologue narrating the subtext. "In order to sell a product or service, you must first make someone believe they are not whole and convince them that your product or service will make them whole." I thought a Business and Communications Degree would better equip me to execute my dreams, yet while studying I never felt inspired, and often reflected on the ethics of what I was being taught.

At school, I used to daydream and fantasize about a much greater mission. I'd dream of changing the world. I'd feel this fire inside of me; an intense a feeling of urgency. I'd look around at my peers playing on Facebook and think to myself that surely there was more to life. I had gone to university in hopes I could tame the fire and unwavering passion to be extraordinary, and find a sense of balance and centre, yet all that seemed to happen was that I became more and more hungry to achieve and experience greatness. I was craving a freedom beyond the confines of university.

The morning before I met my elf-like friend at the vegetarian restaurant I woke up from an intense dream. It was one of many dreams I was having at the time, and struggling to make sense of. I had a dream that I was travelling Australia in a van. I felt like I was going crazy, which was ironic, because it was a constant battle in my own mind to determine whether or not I was. I had suffered from mental illness for the entirety of my teenage years, so there was a strong possibility that what I perceived as my dreams and desires, was actually delusion.

And yet the desires I had to free myself from any 'box' became impossible to ignore. University was not the place for me to explore the unlimited aspects of my own genius or my own expression, I needed to be free, with nothing holding me back. It was an extremely confronting realisation. I didn't want to follow the path that others had followed to unhappiness and stress. I didn't want to throw away my artistic dreams for the "realistic" dreams of climbing a corporate ladder in one of Australia's highest paying advertising or marketing firms. It dawned on me that I needed to take drastic action. I started to understand what desire truly was.

DESIRE IS HOLY

Desire is holy. Think of your basic desires: food, water, sex, shelter. These are necessary for us to desire, because they mean survival for us and our species. This is no different from any other desires you have or and experience. I often see in my work how clients resist discussing their various personal desires; anything from sexual desire to, professional desire, to the desire to move away from their existing life and begin the creation of a new one. There's a fear that surrounds the revelation of desire them. Note that desire is your evolution calling you. We are unconsciously drawn to the things that are going to help us grow and evolve.

Desire is guiding you towards a deeper understanding of yourself, the world, and how you relate to it. To follow our desires is to be in flow with our path. The journey to self-actualisation is a natural process, reached by 'following the path of least resistance.' Or, otherwise simply put, stop fighting yourself, and instead honour your desires and follow your heart. Your evolution is calling you towards total awareness of your wholeness. To suppress your desires is to suppress who it is you really are. Ultimately, when we have fulfilled all of our desires, we can transcend beyond desire. To desire nothing is to understand we are already complete and have no need. This is the journey of awakening, but we find this by listening listen to ourselves, rather than fighting ourselves and suppressing what it is we want.

DESIRE IS NOT YOUR PROBLEM, YOUR JUDGEMENT OF DESIRE IS.

At 18, I walked back through my university library listening to my headphones after dropping an assignment off. A friend called out my name, but I was in my own world; daydreaming- as per usual. To grab my attention, he asked a girl sitting closest to the door to reach out and grab my attention. Before she could, I was stopped in my tracks. It was as if, unexplainably, electricity had hit me. I turned around, the sound of my friend's voice became non-existent in my reality. I went to introduce myself to a girl sitting closest to the door but noticed that I couldn't quite get my words out, so instead, she put her hand out to introduce herself. I went to shake her hand and noticed her looking at the way my hand was shaking. Then she smiled at me; a mischievous kind of smile.

The drowned out voice of my friend suddenly entered the forefront of my consciousness as he asked me to sit down. I picked up a pen that was sitting on the desk and sat staring at the pen, I clicked it repeatedly in an attempt to centre my focus. She started telling me about her assignment, trying to support me in calming down. I began to offer my insight and perspective, entertaining the alibi she had given me to ease into our conversation. After 45 minutes or so, I put the pen down and placed my hand down beside me. She, subtly, moved her hand over so it gently brushed mine. A rush of blood went from my heart straight into my stomach.

My attraction to her was intense. I felt vulnerable. She later asked me to walk her to her car. We walked in silence; the energy between us having a conversation of its own. As we approached her car, she leaned against the driver's door.

"So, I thought you liked boys?"

I replied, "I thought I did too."

"So, what is this?" She asked.

"I don't know," I stuttered.

She replied, "Desire comes in many, many forms when you start to open your mind."

At 18, I had to accept that I had feelings for a girl. I had never considered my sexuality in this way, and it challenged the way I related to myself and the world. My sexuality and sexual expression played a large role, as it does for many 18-year-olds in shaping my way of relating and thinking about gender. Considering the intensity of the attraction, I had no choice but to accept it, and become honest with myself. It fundamentally changed my identity.

It's important to explore and accept, what it is you desire. It's a significant part of the journey to loving yourself, and thus loving out loud.

Here is the space to properly explore this.

What are you attracted to? What do you genuinely resonate with? What do you feel magnetised towards? Your spirit knows the direction you must travel in order to expand. To resist this, because of judgement, is to deny yourself of your true connection to the universe, to yourself, and to those around you. This is a safe space to become honest with yourself. Drop fear for a second. Here are six points which will bring you a greater sense of honesty within yourself.

1. Honour what you are drawn towards and open yourself to another realm of possibility.

Beyond the restrictions of what you believe you should want, exists what you actually want. Only you can be the one to give yourself permission to connect with this, to deeply honour and accept this. What we are attracted to is something that, even in the denial and suppression of it, won't ever disappear. Attraction is designed to be an extremely powerful motivator. There's a power in acting on what we are attracted to, it is intentionally potent to give us enough courage to be proactive.

2. Desire is our heart speaking to us. It knows more than the mind and guides us to different situations that have the power to bring our lives more meaning and fulfilment.

When we are honest with ourselves in what we desire, we become open to situations and experiences that we previously were closed off from. When we step into this newness, into what is initially unfamiliar (and potentially uncomfortable), it expands our horizons, giving greater perspective to explore and learn about ourselves.

3. If everything was neutral, if we had no desire, we wouldn't experience contrast. Without contrast, we wouldn't have experience at all.

If we never felt hunger, what joy would there be in eating? If we never felt physical attraction, what pleasure would we get from sex? If we never desired our wildest dreams, what fulfilment would executing them bring us? It's important to understand that desires are sacred. They give us the opportunity to have a preference, and with preference, we can activate choice. Choice creates a sense of empowerment and self-directedness. To shut down what we desire is to rob ourselves from experiencing the true depth of feeling. We become numb by accepting less than our truth.

4. Stop being afraid that your desires are wrong- truth exists beyond judgement.

Opinions and judgements are entirely subjective. All we have in this life is our own perception, which we have the power to alter and control in every moment. To align our perspective with our true desires brings us into a state of flow. It is within our control whether we allow other people's opinions of what we should or shouldn't want to affect us. We give our power away to others when we put our own desires aside.

When I began to realise that my desire to be creative and entrepreneurial went against the grain of what my family wanted of me, a huge amount of resistance rose up in me. Following my desire in this instance meant a separation from my personal relationships. It would have been impossible to empower myself if I had chosen social acceptance, over remaining strong in my own truth. When I started to say **yes** to myself, I started to notice the way my desires grew. My heart began to yearn for things that seemed increasingly more unconventional. This is when I began to realise how **conditioned we are.** We're taught **what** to want, **what** to think, and **what** to feel, rather than being given the space to connect with **our truth.** The process of saying **yes** to myself did, and continues to, propel me towards my own expansion and evolution.

5. Stop lying to yourself about what you want because you're afraid you don't have the capability of actualising it. If you desire it, it is meant for you.

One thing I live by is the understanding that all of my potential is already inside of me. It's waiting to be discovered, expressed and actualised. The journey is the process of actualising it (loving out loud). When we begin to tap into and connect with our own potentiality, we become increasingly familiar with it. Familiarising yourself with what you know your potential to be, makes it easier to align your choices and actions to that potential. Instead of doubting yourself at the prospect of an opportunity, you can approach opportunities with more confidence. Allowing yourself to be present with your desires (without judgment) is to place your awareness on them. From here, you will begin to notice how they are showing up in your reality. If you keep your awareness on why you can't actualise your desires, it will be reinforced to you. Remember, the brain always aims to prove you right. You are capable of having what you want.

6. The process of creating something in the physical is to first identify it, then to vocalise it (honestly and unashamedly), then to act on it.

Think about what currently exists in your reality, and for a second imagine the whole process of creation is the opposite of what you think it is. Instead of the outside world informing your thoughts of it, it's your thoughts that are informing the outside world. Or at least it's your thoughts informing your experience of the outside world, which is no different as far as you're concerned. You are beyond powerful, there is undeniable evidence of you being the one to command reality with your thoughts. Evolution works through us. The trick is to really **know** this so we can **begin working in partnership with it.** We have the creative control, and the free will, to choose what we experience. However, we first need to become aware that we are already doing this, so we can start to bring awareness to what it is

we truly want.

What do you truly want for your life?

1. *How does your dream reality look?*

2. *What fantasies do you keep locked away?*

3. *What do you desire?*

4. *What do you want to feel?*

What terrifies you about letting go of who you think you are?

Once you've reached a place of total honesty with yourself, acceptance becomes a crucial step in integrating who you are deeper within your truth. You may have found that there's a significant gap between who you were and who you are. We can, understandably, be afraid of letting go of who we think we should be - but this is the time to be courageous.

One of the greatest acts of courage is to practice letting go. A part of this practice is knowing when to shed certain aspects of our identity in order to evolve. There are significant parallels between acceptance and identity.

Acceptance: The agreement to a belief or idea.

Identity: Defining characteristics of a person.

As humans, our innate need for acceptance is one of our key drivers. Maslow's famous hierarchy of needs, which looks at our six fundamental needs, states that acceptance and belonging is one of our most primal needs as humans.

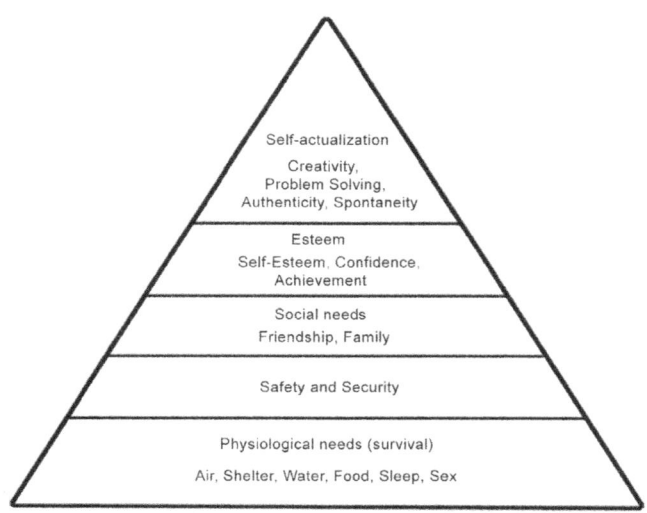

Our need for acceptance and belonging is foundational and, in many ways, must be achieved before we can evolve to new levels of esteem, purpose and actualisation. For this reason, if we feel we have characteristics and elements of our identity that may be rejected by others socially, we tend to reject those parts of ourselves (or at least not show them out loud to other people). This is detrimental because we are then in a constant tension between receiving social acceptance and not being fully seen. This sends a message to our subconscious that we are not worthy of full acceptance. We need to love ourselves enough to honestly express who we are, so we may subsequently experience genuine and authentic acceptance, and thus progress to deeper levels of our awareness and expansion. From that foundation, we can then develop a stronger sense of self-esteem and actualisation.

Most of us have an important distinction between who we are, and who we think we are. It's important that honesty precedes acceptance in this process; there's deep self-acceptance required once you become honest with yourself regarding who you truly are, and what it is you truly want.

The hardest part of recovering from a mental illness is not the understanding that you want something different for yourself. Nor is it necessarily making the changes to your self-talk, or the way you interact with life. It's the separation you experience from your identity. For me, stepping out of the story of anorexia was gut-wrenchingly painful. I had spent five years in agony, each day believing I was getting closer and closer to reaching perfection. Anorexia was the compass for my self-belief, my sense of control, my discipline, and the way other people identified me. I let anorexia root itself in my identity. It dictated and determined my mood, and thus the way I interacted with life. I'd swing from confidence to painful fragility. From feeling an intoxicating high, to feeling inconsolable depression and crushing self-hatred. However, the one point of stability during all the highs and lows was in knowing I had created a point of separation between myself and other people; a way to feel superior, even though it was anchored in extreme feelings of inferiority.

After years of feeling intense pain, with my body breaking down on me, I eventually had to face the truth: "Am I prepared to die for this (eating) disorder, or not?" Deep down, I knew there was more life in me- there were things I wanted to achieve, hidden components of me that needed to be expressed. Anorexia was not worth my life- irrespective of my intense investment in it. Through understanding this it became clear that I had to find a way to overcome the all-consuming fear that came with letting it go. This is when I had to face the hardest hitting questions:

· *"Who am I, if not anorexic?"*
· *"How are people going to see me without my anorexia?"*
· *"Will I be seen as weak for relinquishing control?"*

The hardest questions were rooted in what others would think of me. The beginning of my letting go process began with the understanding that I was enough for myself, irrespective of others' opinions and judgments. The reality is, despite thinking otherwise, most people are far too consumed with their own insecurities to notice yours. Those who are truly self-aware, know the limitations that come with judgment, whether of themselves or others, and are in their own ongoing practice of acceptance. We get tricked; sucked into believing that the material world defines us, when really, our greatest power is remaining in charge of the way we show up in the world. When I learnt to be enough for myself, those around me could only accept the same. Through standing strong in who you are, there's no room to be swayed or influenced, and you give others no choice but to also accept you if they want you in their lives. You become the example of how you wish to be treated.

Starting an organisation at 18 set me apart from my university peers. I had focus, goals and dreams that others struggled to relate to. I was 'outside the box' and struggled to find the level of acceptance I craved from my peers. It was a huge lesson in self-acceptance. If we wait for others' approval, acceptance or permission before beginning our journey, we will never cross the start line - let alone reach the finish line. We need to move beyond needing others' permission and acknowledgement before taking action towards reaching our dreams. If you've been given a vision, only you can see it. There's a significant amount of courage that comes with being enough for yourself and accepting yourself that spurs a crucial self-determination and power that turn your ideas and dreams into a reality. This tension is an important motivation. My understanding of this deepened the more I followed my heart and paved my own path.

At 19, I was in negotiations with a sponsor that would potentially be a game-changing opportunity. I was on the precipice of being able to tour

Australia but still didn't have the deal concreted. With no certainty around the sponsorship, I was having to make a decision around whether or not to defer university. I felt a huge amount of pressure from my friends and family to 'get real,' and remain in my degree. If I deferred, and then didn't get the sponsorship, what was I going to do for eight months? I was going to seem like a fool, putting my life on hold whilst my cohort progressed through their studies. Yet, I couldn't help but be overtaken by another possibility; to actively watch my vision unfold and go on one of the greatest adventures of my life. Surely, I wasn't crazy. Surely all these synchronicities were leading to something. My faith was strong, irrespective of the negativity surrounding me. My family had just called me to reinforce the stupidity of deferring, "education is the most important thing, you should focus on it. There's plenty of time to follow your dreams once you have a solid foundation." How could I possibly explain to them the experiences I had been having? What was guiding me? None of them believed or spoke about a higher power. I knew my truth, though, I could feel it in the way my gut constantly felt like it was set on fire. I couldn't go through another semester watching my peers play on their phones and nod their head every time they were asked a question, practically burning their tuition fees in front of me.

I kept thinking, "That couldn't be it, right? Surely that's not as good as it gets?" Going against these voices of 'reason' was hard, but it felt worse to ignore the feelings in my heart and my gut. Who was I to challenge this? I had nothing behind me as evidence that I was right. The sponsorship may not come through. Nonetheless, the knowing in me was strong enough to trust. That, or I looked at the rest of the world and thought, *"Even if they're right and I'm wrong, I think I'd prefer to be wrong."* I was ready to risk it all for the possibility of living my truth. It had finally clicked.

I HAD TO ACCEPT MYSELF BEFORE ANYONE ELSE COULD.

A pivotal realisation for me was getting to a place where I could handle the thought of trying and potentially failing. The prospect of failure was difficult to come to terms with. Genuine self-acceptance is accepting yourself irrespective of outcomes. I had accepted the fear of failure, I had rehearsed how it would feel for everyone around me to say, *"I told you so,"* and I had accepted myself enough to be okay with it. To know that I would survive it- even if I only had myself. I had come to the point where I didn't need their acceptance, their validation, and most of all, I didn't need their permission. I was doing it for me. To back myself. To love myself. To express myself.

In hindsight, I truly believe this is the point of actualisation I had to reach in order to manifest my breakthrough and my success. I could not have attracted the resources I needed to execute this dream until I had demonstrated to myself that I had enough self-acceptance to be okay with failing and to be okay with the judgments that would surface from my friends and family. I believe that it was because I stepped into this power that the universe delivered to me and the sponsorship came through. As I said earlier, I don't believe in coincidence, nor in luck or chance. It's a process of alignment.

1. Do not wait for permission.

2. People can only accept your authentic self when you express it unapologetically.

3. Failure is the opportunity to deepen self-acceptance and try again with more awareness.

The only real way to ease the pain and anxiety that comes with uncertainty and change is to fiercely accept yourself. Self-acceptance is not a token thing that people say, nor is it a cliché. It's a powerful and extremely bold signal to the world that you can handle anything that comes your way. There's a model I use to remind myself of the power that comes with acceptance.

ACCEPTANCE leads to -

HONEST COMMUNICATION which leads to -

TRUST.

These three have a symbiotic relationship. Without reaching a place of self-acceptance, you won't be able to maintain a consistent degree of honesty with yourself. Acceptance is the ingredient that allows you to be grounded in a deep honesty with yourself, and thus others. Without acceptance, it will feel as though you are ducking and weaving from the aspects of yourself that you don't accept and love. Denial leaves holes; blind spots in the truth, which is a trick our minds play on us to avoid pain. Your mind is programmed to avoid pain because (once upon a time) pain meant a threat to your survival. Yet, without pain and discomfort, growth is impossible. Once you have a relationship with yourself built on complete honesty, you begin to trust yourself. You know that you're not afraid to front up to the truth of situations, irrespective of the consequence. You can trust that you will take the high road, instead of the easy road.

We lose trust in ourselves when we begin to compromise what it is we truly want or need as a way to gain the love and acceptance of others. We create the illusion that we need others' love and acceptance at any cost because, in these moments, we are failing to provide it to ourselves. When you dim your light for the love of someone else, or to fit in, you send a message to yourself that you aren't loveable as you are. This will grind away at your level of self-acceptance, and over time, your trust in yourself. You won't feel strong in your discernment of situations, or your opinion of others' character. And, the cycle will continue.

Seeing all situations and relationships beyond your own needs builds a strong foundation within yourself. To see the world as a mirror of yourself is to draw empowered conclusions around what you want and what you don't want. This needn't be in a judgmental way, it's a simple process of choosing what you prefer, and would prefer, to be experiencing.

DRAWING CONCLUSIONS.

Have you ever thought about the expression 'drawing conclusions?' It insinuates that we can only ever create our own conclusions, which we draw to make our choices easier. I want to show you a different way of capitalising on your decision-making process. We choose the way we frame things in our world. Meaning is completely subjective, and in knowing this it gives us the power to choose what things mean to us. The frame in which you see life determines the quality of your experience. Instead of drawing a thousand lines in the sand, here is a way to narrow down your choices into two categories:

LOVE or FEAR.

Love's nature is continually expansive- it will keep expanding beyond time and space. It has a magical way of transmuting barriers into possibilities. Fear is a force that is designed to separate and restrict us. A fearful mind is often ripe with judgements. Love's natural consequence is to accept. Think back to the first time you fell in love; seeing the perfection in someone for the first time. The feeling of being able to bring the stars to earth, the feeling of being able to draw a whole future in front of your eyes. The feeling of not being able to wait a second longer to see that person. This feeling is self-generated. Although we experience this affection for another, we experience it within ourselves. This feeling exists inside of us- as do all feelings. When we fall in love, we meet an activator of this love- we see ourselves more clearly in them, which then contributes to the feelings of being understood, of safety, and of familiarity. Of course, they're familiar, they are you! They match the parts of yourself you have already accepted and loved. This is an experience we can have with every single person, but first, we need to explore our inner-world so that the camera lens that is the outside world can move into focus. When we're in a state of fear, we tend to want to be conservative and not throw ourselves into full expression. It's a survival state.

OVERCOMING BIAS

Bias is the undercover agent of fear, it's what stops us seeing our reflection in others. We focus on the seemingly vast difference between us and others; skin colour, nationality, sexuality, education, social status. All of which are medial and insignificant compared to the aspects of us that make us the same; our humanity, the love inside each of us. These biases will sometimes trick us into believing we are separate from others. It is fear's nature to separate us from each other, to have us remain individual. Love is the unifier, the thing that bridges the gaps between us and all things.

Rumi said it: *"Love is the bridge between us and everything."*

Humans seek connection. We want to remember our humanity, and in order to do this, we must strive to be in a deep state of acceptance and love for one another. If you find yourself judging yourself, or another person, ask yourself: What would love do?

In beginning to understand love's nature, and by familiarising yourself with love, you become more able to understand how love would make decisions. I often ask this as a trigger question when I feel stuck or unable to make choices, in particular, if I feel I'm in a state of anger, irritation or judgement. This question allows me to ground back into conscious decision making. There's a big power that comes from learning to respond to the world rather than react.

Fear is reactive, love is responsive.

Becoming conscious of the way fear plays out in your reality is also a really great way to move closer to love. It will help you become aware when fear is leading your decision making and framing the way you see life, and with this awareness, you'll have the power to move toward love. Often fear is the reason we remain stuck in life, unable to progress forward. In order to be graceful in the way we navigate change, there's a necessary shift in your thinking that needs to take place; from judgment and bias to acceptance. Our biases and prejudices often prevent us from seeing the truth in situations and block us from learning. We can't necessarily stop having biases, but we can become more aware of them, as to not be dedicated to by them. For example, if you asked me to give you an opinion of this book, as the author, I can't help but have a bias. I have an investment in its success and am too involved in it to eliminate my bias. Having said this, through awareness, I can give an objective perspective of the quality of writing and the content. By remaining objective, I have a much better chance of being able to create a better quality book, because I won't be so averse, or afraid, to look at the flaws. This awareness is extremely powerful.

Take the time to answer these few questions:

1. What biases do you have?

2. Where do you feel prejudice towards something?

3. What is the fear that rises in you regarding what is different or unfamiliar?

ACCEPTANCE ALLOWS YOU TO CHANGE AND EVOLVE

Once you begin to work through some of your judgments and become more at peace with yourself and others, you won't have the barriers holding you back and blocking you from expanding. Change is often a daunting thing for people to experience. I've noticed a big correlation in my work between people that experience symptoms of poor mental health, and simultaneously trying to manage a big life change. When you're presented with the need for change in your life it can be terrifying, but why? Is it really all down to fear of the unknown? In many instances, it's due to the loss of an identity. Through acceptance we make peace with ourselves and our past. Instead of looking at chapters of our lives and thinking, "Was this all for nothing, if I now have to move on?" we understand that change is a natural part of life.

There are a few premises that help to navigate and stay calm through the process of change.

1. All experiences are impermanent.

2. Although we can't keep our physical circumstances forever, we hold the wisdom of all they've taught us.

3. We always have ourselves.

Once we accept these things, we become more graceful in our navigation of life; we get better at letting go and owning our stories. The trick is to find the inner joy of play; of creativity. When it is time to move on we have an opportunity for recreation. We never lose our past, it will always come with us into the present moment. I see it more like a kaleidoscope, the process of changing how it looks, but never our pieces. We have the power to choose what our past means to us, and to decide whether to pay attention to the lessons life is giving us, or remain stuck in the same unconscious cycles again and again. Often, once we have learnt what we need to progress forward in our own level of evolution, we reach a level of mastery within our existing circumstances, which will start to manifest as symptoms of "outgrowing your life situations." This can include, places, people, jobs, hobbies, or really any area of your life. You'll feel this through feelings of restlessness, potential irritation, boredom, complacency, a feeling of "same shit, different day." It's important to listen closely to this resistance, because to ignore it is to miss the opportunity to consciously participate in your own evolution; and life will begin shifting and changing things for you.

LETTING GO AND IDENTITY

During my recovery from anorexia it was crucial to begin hypothesising an identity which integrated the characteristics that anorexia fulfilled within me, whilst finding a healthier and more productive avenue to demonstrate and channel those characteristics. For me these characteristics included:

· Self-control/regulation
· Focus
· Personal power
· Determination

When I broke this down, I realised these are all actually extremely desirable traits, and should be integral to the new version of myself I was creating. I realised that, with these traits harnessed for their power and used for the progression- rather than the destruction, of myself, I had the ability to work towards anything I wanted. In essence, the strength that came with denying myself of a human need; food, was powerful enough to achieve anything.

The more that I saw the creative power that we have, the more I understood that the majority of us are bound within social constructions and 'norms' simply because we don't think to question them. When you start to become 'self-made' (and by that, I mean, begin consciously creating yourself and your life), you see immediate evidence that we are designing our realities with our thoughts, words, and actions. The more confident you become in your own process, the more your heart will start desiring after bigger and seemingly obscure dreams. You begin to separate yourself from the pressures of conformity; and through that liberation, start to connect to your unique path.

Once I had broken free of conforming to the path others were pushing me towards, I found a new sense of liberation, and with that came access to much more creativity. My imagination started daring to dream bigger. I found myself imagining the impossible and completely believing it was possible. Once you accept failure, everything becomes possible.

GET REALLY GOOD AT FAILING.

It's extremely important to change your relationship with failure. There's a cliché I always refer to: F.A.I.L = First Attempt In Learning. Often, because we base our worth and value on achievement, and being seen as successful, we experience failure in a definitive way. It triggers all of our insecurities and fears, and we struggle to remain in a state of self-acceptance. For this reason, we stop taking risks and seclude ourselves to our comfort zone. The problem with this is that there's no room to grow inside your comfort zone. Growth will only begin to happen once you're uncomfortable and through, this you'll have the opportunity to access deeper insights.

I've come to understand that many people don't want to step outside their comfort zone because they are crippled by the prospect of failing. Self-acceptance, and accepting that failure is a natural by-product of mastering something, gives you the power to change your relationship with failure. For me, now, failure is the process of learning. I don't require other people's validation or acceptance, which brings me an incredible sense of freedom, and freedom of expression.

Ask yourself;

1. What is your current relationship with failure?

2. How do you currently define success?

3. How can you reframe success and failure to empower, rather than disempower yourself?

There's no greater freedom than the feeling of not needing others' approval.

When I first realised I was attracted to a girl, I experienced a lot that came up within me. Aside from the opinions and potential judgement I may experience from those closest to me, these feelings also made me re-evaluate how I related to myself; in fact, my entire identity.

Yet, I was experiencing love. I've often asked myself how and why love can sometimes hurt. How can something so beautiful, and so natural, sometimes be met with so much judgement? How could we compartmentalise love into okay and not okay? Self-acceptance was a crucial lesson through this process.

What I've come to understand about love is that it's designed to grow us. Love is designed to bring up, and trigger, the fear in you because it's our growth path. When we judge our experiences, especially of love, we disengage ourselves from its learning pathway. Without triggers, there's no reason, or way, to inquire more deeply into our experience, and expand ourselves. The pain we experience in love is our greatest opportunity to grow. The depth of the pain is the equal distance of opportunity we have to grow *(when we know how to harness and channel that pain into our evolution)*.

Love will bring up all things, because love is all things. Finding peace in love is learning the process of regulation; to show up for love in the wisest, and most mature way- which requires full personal responsibility. It's a misconception that love will always be seamless, because our perception and relationship with ourselves play such a fundamental role in how we experience love. Love IS always seamless; however, it is a wild ride to awaken to the seamlessness of love. We must become the observers of our experiences of love; the triggers that arise in us through being loved, and through offering love to the world; and bring consciousness and deep understanding and acknowledgement to them so that we have a more conscious choice in how we're showing up for love, through our behaviour. This is the process of articulation. To Love Out Loud, literally. Our love is always inside of us. The journey is not about 'finding it', it's about expressing it, or 'actualising it'; that is to say, realising it.

Literal meaning:

Real : Real, Ise: (a suffix meaning TO SEE). Realise = to see the real.

This is the process of 'undoing' or 'being', rather than seeking, finding or doing. The enlightening moment is when you realise and accept that you are enough. The enlightening moment is when you realise that you are love, and that you always have been, and always will be love. Once we awaken to this, we understand that it is only ever our perception that is distorted, and never our true selves. The gift in this, more than anything, is the power that it provides us to accept that our perception is changeable and malleable; to know that we have control over how we experience the world, others and ourselves (therefore how we experience love).

How are you managing love inside of yourself? If you take full responsibility for what comes up in you, in the face of love, then you are in the driver's seat of how you can grow through it. And, this can only be achieved through complete acceptance.

When I returned from my three-month trip to South America and came home to my girlfriend, there was much tension within the relationship. There was the truth of how we felt, yet neither of us had the ability to see beyond the pain we were both experiencing. There was so much judgement that prevented us from accepting the reality of our situation, making it impossible for us to progress. The people in our lives had strong opinions around whether or not we should remain together. It's an incredibly painful tension; the tension behind the truth of the love you know in your heart, and your ability to express and actualise this. It was, ultimately, this relationship that inspired me to write this book. The essence of the love we experienced became the fuel and the insatiable curiosity that inspired me to break love down in a way that could be better understood. Love is such a force to be reckoned with, yet very often it's hard to fully embrace and accept.

There were moments I would look at her and feel the most incredible, overwhelming and frightening fragility. When you feel these levels of vulnerability, so much fear tends to rise in you, and often an impulse to run away or deny the love. Yet, it's this love that makes the ordinary so extraordinary. The moments she wouldn't even realise I was watching her, and I'd be filled with so much love. Handling this amount of emotion can be difficult when you're inexperienced or unsure of how to manage and regulate it. From the outside, it was easy to pass off as incompatibility, or that we were simply not meant to be together. The reality was that we were both in pain, and unsure of how to resolve it. Our fights became more and more aggressive, and harder to reconcile. I have never seen this as not loving each other. We can't know hate until we know love, and that line is often fragile. Through all of our arguments and blame, what we were actually communicating was such a deep need to be heard, and to be seen. We were blinded by ourselves, and unable to see each other. The deep need for acknowledgement often makes it difficult to accept situations with so much emotional charge, yet without this, it's impossible to resolve situations and progress forward.

It was this truth that made me question love deeply. I couldn't just let this relationship go and move on, I was committed to coming to a place of acceptance. There was an eternity in that love, and it is still is the fuel that assists in creating my future. Accepting the pain, as opposed to running away and trying to avoid, became an incredibly powerful motivator in my world. Often when situations don't meet our exact expectations, we want to completely deny that there was ever truth at all. I started to learn and accept that love can take many forms. It's up to us to accept our reality and refocus the love and our experiences into something new.

Acceptance is the final stage of part one in your transformation. Once you have reached a place of complete acceptance, something remarkable happens. You reach a point of challenge. Acceptance, by nature, cannot be penetrated and there are no more lessons your past experiences can teach you. From here, the process enters a creation phase; that involves relinquishing your identity as it stands, and designing a new one with more conscious ability to direct your vision.

Congratulations, and welcome to part two.

PART *TWO*

INTRODUCTION

Now that we've mastered where we were, how about where we're going? What needs to happen between the 'then', and the 'there'? Through acceptance, you can awaken to the now. There are no longer hooks of regret, pain or judgment dragging you back into your past. Isn't the present moment expansive? Can you feel its infinite nature pulsating through you? There are some things you need to know about the present moment.

The present moment has no attachment to anything.

And as a result of having no attachment to anything, it's in a space of complete surrender at all times. It's willing to die, in all moments. That sounds a little intense, but it's actually one of its most magic superpowers. The ability to let go is the superpower that activates your limitlessness. The more you let go, the more space you have to seduce everything you desire. This is an important distinction:

SURRENDER IS CRUCIAL IN MEETING OUR DESIRES

We can desire things and still surrender our expectations of them. These two concepts seem a little counterintuitive, right? How can you completely surrender be non-attached, and yet still desire things?

Desire is a force that comes from deep within you. It's sacred. It's the way your spirit communicates with you in an attempt to evolve itself. When you're truly connected, your desires are not egoic. They no longer come from your ego-mind attempting to attach itself to tangible things to validate its existence out of fear. True desires are deeply rooted in love and joy. Your spirit has no fear as to whether or not you're good enough to live the life you desire. On the other side of fear is love, right? And the nature of love is unconditional; it holds no conditions, and therefore no attachments.

There's a significant difference between apathy, or "not giving a fuck", and holding no attachment to something. All love has to do is seek more of itself (which is expressed through *your hearts desires)*.

Your ego will disguise temptation with desire in extremely convincing ways, and it takes a lot of self-awareness and discernment to differentiate between the two. There are useful ways to practice this discernment.

Ask yourself

1. *Does this feel expansive, free, and light?*

2. *Would I feel completely comfortable being honest about this?*

3. *Is it free of the shackles of guilt and shame? (Really feel into this, because often another's judgment of us make us feel unnecessary and unwarranted guilt/shame. Really judge this against your (and only your) truth).*

4. *Where in my body do I feel this temptation/desire? Is it heart-based?*

When you know you are living from your truth, it becomes far easier to surrender. The key understanding in awakening to this is that death is not only physical, it happens many times throughout our lives. Becoming conscious of this gives you more opportunities in directing and designing your re-birthing process.

(LOL) Love **OUT LOUD**

What are you willing to die for?

Romance, as a concept, has its origins rooted in a heroic journey. There are many connotations of romance and pain; the sting of love, to experience pain for a lover makes the reconciliation so much sweeter- think of Romeo and Juliet. Did the forbidden nature of their love not also drive the intensity of their romance? I see death in this way. Doesn't the ultimate reality, and certainty, of death, not make life so much sweeter and more meaningful?

As humans, we require juxtaposition. We need polarity, contrast, and variety. Without this juxtaposition, we could not have experience;

experience is birthed through contrast. We can only exist in relation to other things. Therefore, to exist in relation to other things, is to have difference, to experience a tension. It is this tension that allows us to have choice. A tension exists between our most favourite and our least favourite meal. A tension exists between how fit we are, and how fit we want to be. It is through experiencing this tension that we have preference. It is crucial to have things we like, and things we don't like, things that annoy us, and things that fill us with joy. If our lives were only ever easy, we would already be at our destination. Juxtaposition, polarity and contrast allow us to experience fulfilment; the tension between these experiences creates the joy in our breakthroughs.

WE ARE IN RELATIONSHIP TO ALL THINGS

It is our responsibility to choose the way we relate to the world, and it is our perception that determines the way we relate.

Relate: To make or show a connection between.

On this note, I have a hard-hitting question for you: *How do you relate to death?*

Perhaps death isn't something you've thought about, or contemplated, yet. However, with the understanding of death, comes a profound opportunity to create meaning. Knowing that you will die one day brings an impermanence to every single thing we experience, and without this, nothing would have meaning.

TENSION CREATES MEANING

Throughout history, Rite of Passage ceremonies across many cultures, specifically Coming Of Age ceremonies, have had one significant factor in common: the confrontation, or realisation, of one's mortality. Why? It is within the confrontation of death that life begins to have meaning. This was facilitated in many ways, usually always using a 'separation from one's comfort zone' as a way to make the adolescent feel a sense of fear and challenge. Overcoming this fear was followed by an immense celebration, organised by the community. Through this tension the young person could grow and step more meaningfully into their responsibilities as an adult. They developed a broader perspective.

We have many examples of how confrontation of death has shaped incredible people in our society today. One example is Tracy Morgan, a famous comedian and actor, who was involved in a multi-car crash in 2014 and almost lost his life. During his ten-day coma, he experienced near death. He discussed meeting his dad and having a conversation with God- who both told him it was not his time. During an interview with Oprah, he said, "I'm now a changed man and that has transformed me for the better." He explained how he now looks at his relationships in a new light. When asked by Oprah on Super Soul Sunday if a person can ever be normal again after a near-death experience, Morgan answered, "No. I told my wife that the other day. 'Something's different. The way I am with people.' I find myself saying 'I love you' two hundred times a day to strangers. I don't care. I don't have to know you to love you! That's how we're supposed to be as human beings. We're supposed to take care of each other."

Tracy Morgan is only one of many, many influential figures who has had a confrontation with death in common. Elizabeth Taylor, a British-American actress and humanitarian, is another who experienced going to the fringes of life. During an interview with Larry King, she discussed her near-death experience during a surgery where she claimed to have left her body. She described passing through a tunnel towards a brilliant white light and encountering the spirit of her third husband who was killed in a plane crash in 1958, whom she referred to as her great love. She had wanted to stay in heaven with Todd, she said, but he had told her that she had work and life ahead of her, and he "pushed me back to my life." Her eleven-person medical team had pronounced her dead and then witnessed her resurrection. She claimed that it was her third husband's love during their encounter that gave her the strength to return to waking life. She explained that she was no longer afraid of death, as she had now experienced it.

The incredible Steve Jobs, co-founder of Apple, revealed his unique relationship with death towards the end of his life, claiming he always had a sense or feeling that he was going to die young. Jobs was a Zen Buddhist and committed vegan, who had a lot to say on the subject of death. In fact, he used 'death' as a motivational force throughout his entire life. Each day he would get up, look in the mirror and ask himself this question:

"If today were the last day of my life, would I want to do what

I'm about to do today?"

And whenever the answer had been "No" for too many days in a row, he would know that he needed to change something. Jobs had successfully mastered the tension between life and death to his advantage, allowing the tension to become an evolutionary pull, rather than a source of disempowerment. Job's final words were, "Oh wow, oh wow, oh wow!" What more of a mark could there be of a satisfied soul?

Jobs read *An Autobiography of a Yogi* every year of his life, encouraging all others to read the book.

Here is a quote from the book: "You must not let your life run in the ordinary way; do something that nobody else has done, something that will dazzle the world." - Paramahansa Yogananda

Ultimately, the relationship between life and death can only be described as *a romance*. The tension that life and death bring to one another provides for us an extremely sacred opportunity to live with true meaning. Our ultimate physical death, however, is not the only death we experience in life. This is a very important thing to understand and become consciously aware of; we will encounter many figurative deaths in our life. Some cultures and people consider these "ego deaths", which is ultimately a shedding of one identity, and a rebirth into a new identity.

I'm sure you've heard this many times before; "Time is our most precious commodity." It makes sense, considering the only thing certain in our life is the fact that it will end one day. All of existence has a finite nature. How is death defined, though? How do *you* define death?

The dictionary defines death as, "a permanent ending", which brings a different perspective. It brings a perspective of what death truly means and provides a different context to its nature. Life itself is not the only thing that is impermanent, or 'finite' - because the very fact that this all ends, insinuates that all singular experiences are impermanent. Yes, this means dark times are impermanent, as are times of affluence, times of popularity, and times of success. For this reason, it's important to not be attached to a single version of self.

We see this cyclical nature in everything. Just because the forest gets burnt, and the trees turn to ashes, does not mean the forest is gone forever.

Just because the flowers and leaves fall in autumn, does not mean the trees will never bloom again. Death happens so that a rebirth can also happen. This can be traced to the most micro of acts; our inhale and exhale. For us to breathe out, we must let go of our inhale, our inhale must 'die'. Similarly, for the inhale to be reborn, we must surrender our exhale. Breath is the life-force of all existence, and it surrenders its life every moment. It demonstrates complete humility through its ability to let go; to not fear death. Learning this through meditation and yoga has always inspired me to ask the question: how could something be so life-giving by surrendering itself so easily to death?

It's only through the acceptance of death that we may truly know what it means to live. Only through letting go, can we truly see what is real and meant for us. Ourselves, as we are in this moment, are dead in the following moment. Life is defined by death, just as death is defined by life. To be eternal is to never experience what it is to be alive, for life has no meaning or value. Only through an ending can a beginning exist, and only through a birth, can life be born.

The ancient understanding of rite of passage is rooted in relinquishing your identity and allowing a great challenge to evoke a rebirth inside of you; a radical transformation. Commonly known as an 'ego death.' It can be hard to see this in today's climate with "self" and independence being the greatest markers of success. In reality, our identities are designed to change our lives. Surrendering, and practising non-attachment can be an extremely joyful experience. An inability to let go can be the root of all suffering. We attach to our identities so deeply that for the most part, we cannot see beyond, or beneath, our own mask. Ironically, those who go through the most extreme versions of an 'ego death', a relinquishing of the self, are seen to be the spiritual masters and leaders in eastern cultures. It is interesting to note that they also experienced many signs of what we would call 'psychosis' before this radical transformation occurred. As a western culture, we put so much significance on individuality and identity, we often struggle to see the beauty in letting go.

I want you to expand your understanding of death. It is not only a physical death that we will experience in our lives but many figurative deaths. To understand and look to death with grace, is to live life with no resistance and complete engagement and participation.

LIFE AND DEATH ARE IN A ROMANCE WITH EACH OTHER

Ultimately, life and death need each other. It can be likened to any relationship between opposites. We're led to believe that it is a relationship between good and bad, when in actual fact, both are equally as important. When we can overcome our fear of death, we experience a sense of wholeness, often described as "oneness", because we awaken to a reality beyond the self. We experience who we are beyond our perceived limitations. Our identities often block us, and limit us, from seeing what else there is to us. We choose the things that we identify with and thus can influence and control both the way we relate to the world, and the way we're perceived by others.

DEATH AND IDENTITY

Identities follow a cycle of life and death, also. Relinquishing your identity, allowing an identity to be shed in order to recreate (or *rebirth*) yourself, is an incredibly powerful process. I've experienced this at several times in my life. The most intense was during my mental illness. My identity was challenged so deeply by the darkness in my mind, there was a gaping void between what my mind was telling me and the rest of those in my world. How could I trust in the words of those around me when their perspective felt so foreign? How can you trust someone who you struggle to relate to? How can you ever really trust someone else's words, over the voice in your own head? Questioning your perception of reality is a scary process. I would shut down or lash out when someone tried to express to me that there was another way. I was loyal to my pain, for the pain was such a strong part of my identity, I had invested so much of myself into that pain, who was I going to be if I let it go?

Imagine if the inhale thought this about itself. Imagine if the inhale refused to let go so that the exhale could never live. How painful that would be to experience (try it; continue to inhale, without allowing yourself to exhale). We believe it's the letting go of our identity that causes us pain, when in fact it's the attachment to it that creates suffering. It was not my potential that was causing me pain, it was my unwillingness to let go of my eating disorder.

My psychologist at the time would say to me, "Nicole, you are not your story." This never made much sense to me as a sixteen-year-old. How was I not my mental illness? It was what I was experiencing, after all. At the time, I didn't understand that we are not what we experience - we are so much more than the story we tell ourselves. As I started to heal, and finally began letting go of my eating disorder, I wrote this in my journal:

"You are so much more than your story. You are love, you are infinite, you are freewill in motion, you are the author of your destiny, holding the pen in all moments and choosing what it is you write onto your page, choosing how the next chapter will unfold- you are not a victim to dogma, you have the power to think freely and write as creatively as you wish. Is this the best idea you have of yourself?"

Although I had glimpses of this wisdom, it only truly and wholly landed when I met someone who I fell madly in love with. I knew from early on that experiencing the love I had with her was forever going to change me. Who I was before we met was gone, I was never going to be the same. The love literally 'killed me', and I was reborn into a fuller expression of myself. This is the true power of love. Hence why people say this love 'brought me to life' or 'woke me up or 'love turned my world on its head.'

Rumi's most famous quote, "Find what you love, and slowly let it kill you." is profound on so many levels... What could bring life more meaning than to consume the hours you have on this incredible planet with the things you love? The truth is that discovering what you're willing to die for is the only way you can discover what is truly worth living for.

The nature of love is that it is designed to recreate you.

It's designed to kill you; its sheer, potent transformational nature infects your body from the inside out. Once you fall in love, you will never be the same person you were beforehand.

LOVER'S ARE OUR GREATEST MIRRORS, AND GREATEST OPPORTUNITY FOR GROWTH

Romantic relationships are one of the key catalysts of transformation. To fall in love is to suddenly have your priorities reorder themselves, and to re-evaluate your direction. When you fall in love with someone, it will often involve a 'letting go' process; letting go of your ideas and expectations around what you thought love would be. As a society, we have many ideas about romantic relationships. We've been sold ideas by Hollywood and Walt Disney around what true love is and what true love should look like; the story that we can only be whole when a Prince, or Princess Charming, comes to save us. Love is far less about what you can get from the other, and far more about our ability to practice loving. Lovers are, for the most part, the most significant mirror of our own self-love.

Romance is made up of our continuous devotion and commitment to nurturing the connection, and to remaining engaged in our own process around what our relationships are teaching us. When both parties are taking responsibility for the relationship, there's an opportunity for love to flourish. Communication is key when deepening your understanding of each other's process. Quite often, this takes patience and humility. Learning to hold space for each other without judgment, or without making it personal, is an incredible gift we offer one another. This life is a process of continually evolving, growing and learning, and relationships are our opportunity to assist each other in navigating life. If you can learn to go through changes with each other, it builds an incredibly strong foundation for each other.

Relationships are often most threatened when a partner, or both partners, begin to grow in different directions. During these times, without the skills to know how to communicate and bridge the expanding distance between each other, there is a lot of room for the relationship to become rocky. When growth is happening between two people; views, beliefs and desires all begin to change, and not always will they continue to align. Acceptance is crucial in order to have a healthy and respectful relationship, so as to not jeopardize or sabotage each other's growth.

It is possible to have a significant amount of love between you and another person, and yet for the gap in your path of growth to become irreconcilable in a point in time. When you have two souls, who are each on their unique path - and both staying true to themselves, it's very possible that without one sabotaging the truth of their own path, they won't be able to continue to share time and space. Our human impulse to possess others and control the direction of our lives and the course of our relationships can be the defining factor that creates toxicity. Often true love means loving from a distance, so the right space can be created for both parties to grow and flourish. When you try and force the wrong puzzle pieces to fit together, it creates an incongruent picture. When we try and control the flow of our journey with another person, we disconnect from the natural symbiosis we have in relationships. Every relationship you form with another will follow its own current; it's a beautiful thing to learn how to respond to one another, rather than react. When we can let go of our expectations and judgments, and be in surrender in the relationship, then we are guided to a space of grace and ease. Here, we are given moments of beautiful, profound love, and to let these go, is to allow new moments, and new versions, of this feeling to emerge. When we try to keep someone close at the expense of their freedom (or ours), it changes the relationship dynamic from that of love to that of fear.

LOVE IS FREEDOM, FEAR IS CONTROL

"When you love someone, set them free."

Love doesn't fear loss, love is ever present even when we aren't sharing a physical space with someone. It's the only force that knows no bounds; time, space, or any conditions. To bring fear into a love-based relationship is to taint the love. I often see it like this: Love is an equal balance of support and challenge. We need to be able to support those we love, as well as confront and challenge them. When we only experience support and agreement, this can lead to a co-dependency. Conversely, when we only experience challenge, the relationship can become abrasive and abusive. Being able to love consciously and healthily is bringing balance into the dynamic.

My idealistic views earlier on in life were very much shaped by Hollywood's ideas of "love saving the day," which is really a watered-down version of reality. Love is an incredibly powerful activator, which takes work to truly navigate and nurture consciously.

It's so important to understand that others don't complete us. We can only realise our wholeness through understanding that what others activate in us is a mirror of ourselves. Relationships are designed to mirror us, so we may increase our self-awareness. When someone leaves you, they cannot take parts of you. Even though you feel loss, when you lose something, you do not lose even an inkling of your worth.

At 21 I met the love of my life. The muse for this book. The person I had the most incredible euphoria with, as well as the most debilitating arguments. On meeting her, things finally made sense. I had an experience of what it felt like to completely lose myself in love. The moment we told each other, 'I love you,' I felt the sensation of everything I had ever lost, everything that had ever hurt me, being wiped from my memory. I felt an incredibly deep sense of gratitude for my whole journey, because it had led me to that moment, and that moment was perfect. It was (one of) my awakenings to love. It was the perfect moment of recognising, through her, the love that had always been inside of me. She was the reflection of me that I had spent so long searching for. Adrenaline filled my body, electricity pulsed through every part of my spirit. It was unlike anything I could've hypothesised, or imagined. At the time I thought she was the only place in the universe that was designed for me; my soulmate who I had found to awaken me to everything I had known and believed in, but never experienced.

After knowing each other for six or so months, I was sitting across from her at a bar as we shared a drink. It was moving into winter, and there was a cool breeze, as I voiced how she had been irritating me a lot. It was a feeling I hadn't been able to place; an itch I hadn't been able to scratch, a feeling I didn't have a name for. It was like a fire constantly burning inside of me, without me understanding how to tame it or recognise what it was rooted in. All I knew was the spirit in me saying, 'Yesssss.' My spirit knew it, even though my conscious mind couldn't yet recognise it as love. How could it? Our minds are exhausted, so overworked and contaminated by millions of messages. It can be so easy to let love pass us by out of sheer ignorance. Only our hearts and our spirits truly know the direction of love, hence why love can often seem so illogical and irrational. Our mind is the servant that must be tamed and taught to be a translator for us. We need to trust in a feeling, though it is completely intangible and undefinable, to guide us more closely to a cognitive understanding of love.

"I think you're in love with me," she said. The words echoed through my entire body, piercing me as though I had suddenly become hollow. The resonance of these words shattered all my misconceptions of what I had previously thought love was. It was a moment in time that I could never go back from; it redefined and recreated me. This was the beginning of a radical journey in understanding love's nature.

This was also one of the first times that I rea.ised that love is physical, as much as it's emotional and spiritual. It has a physical resonance. It was literally like 'lightning had struck me.' The experience of losing myself in love over the next two years taught me so much about what it meant to have a balanced, stable and healthy relationship. I became so attached to the love that I lost sight of the love that existed inside of me. Love has just as much to teach us through the letting go process as it does through the process of falling in love. I believe in the term "love is a drug"; we need to be aware and careful of how we interact with it. The very action of love requires the practice of balance and acceptance - instead of grasping it and wanting to control or possess it.

Learning to practice non-attachment is not being detached. It's allowing things to be as they are, without wanting to control them. The acceptance and deeper realisation of death and what it means, allows us to be in a completely receptive state. This is because all fear is ultimately rooted in the fear of death. The fear of being hurt, heartbroken or rejected, all come back to our evolutionary biology that states, "To be in pain, or out of a comfort zone, or rejected by the tribe, is a direct threat to my life." Which, 10,000 years ago, was the reality. Fear is an instinct designed to keep us alive, yet in modern-day society, there are very few threats to our life, and this same instinct prevents us from experiencing, growing and thriving when it's subconscious.

Transforming your unconscious relationship with fear into a conscious relationship is extremely powerful This fear is the same tension that provides us with both awareness and growth. I believe in this so much that I won't work toward visions or projects that I don't experience some type of fear towards. When I feel this, I know the vision is big enough to challenge and grow me.

The experience of love is naturally going to bring up fear because of the vulnerability associated with love. If we haven't been supported in the past and held in our vulnerability, this will feel even more difficult to move past. The fear is encouraging you to move away from something that has previously caused you pain, because that is how we are wired. Your brain and your nervous system are designed to assist you in avoiding pain. These past experiences, associations and commitments we've made to ourselves, for example; "I will never let someone hurt me again" or "I will never open my heart to someone again," have a real-life impact on our present-moment experiences of love. These experiences create baggage that stop us from receiving love.

In intense moments of love, we open ourselves fully, inviting love into our hearts. If we begin to doubt the experience, we close ourselves off and begin to resist it. This creates blockages and prevents us from accessing love. This doubt directs our focus towards the barriers- which are rooted in fear, as, opposed to focussing on the receiving of love. As much as there are shades of grey, being receptive and open to love is a case of black and white. You're either open, or you're not. If you're impacted and triggered, and therefore taken away from the experience of unconditional love, then you are in a closed state. This is not something to judge, but rather to hold an awareness of, so that you can move back into a state of receptivity.

I encourage you to ask yourself, **"Am I closed to love?"**

Take the time to journal some reflections on this, asking yourself, "What fears are you holding? What are you most triggered by?". By becoming consciously aware of when you shut down, you then have the ability to work through the trigger and come back to a place of openness. Self-reflection is so important when it comes to this process. Throughout this book, you'll be more and more deeply initiated into a receptive relationship with love, which is ultimately a reflection of yourself.

TRIGGERS ARE THE GIFT OF AWARENESS

When you're struggling to find balance in a relationship, often it's because the relationship is, in some way, triggering you.

Triggers show us the areas we are yet to accept, and love, in ourselves.

I see triggers as the breaking of our expectations; when we want something to be a certain way but it shows up differently. For example, when we want our partner to acknowledge our efforts at planning a date, and they don't. Or when we want our partner to clean the house, and they don't. We create expectations in our mind that hold the conditions of our acceptance; and unless these expectations are met, we struggle to accept the reality of the situation.

A process that's helped me ground myself whilst triggered is this;

1. Pause and breathe

It's important to recognize that when you're triggered, you've reverted straight back to your reptilian brain. Here you can't make rational choices. You need to stop, calm down and regulate yourself, in order to be more objective.

2. Step out of your story momentarily

Analyse what the narrative is that you're telling yourself. For example, "They **never** support me," or "They don't love me." When our emotions are spiked, it's often easy to dramatize and exaggerate the situation in your mind. Simply **acknowledging** your emotions is a powerful way to diffuse them.

3. Analyse your situation objectively

Once you've calmed down (which may require stepping away from the situation completely for a period of time), try to look at the situation objectively and see where you were being reactive.

4. Look for the gifts and lessons in your situation

What was the trigger? Have a look at what this trigger was highlighting for you. What new awareness can you find within this trigger? What needs or wants are you now aware of that you weren't before?

5. Reconcile the situation

Re-approach the situation responsively. Own your emotion and trigger, and provide the space for the other person to reflect and share theirs. Often no outcome is necessary, rather a mutual acknowledgement of each other's process and feelings.

6. Self-Reflection and growth

With this new self-awareness, have a look at how you can strengthen and deepen your capacity to accept and love a situation beyond your expectations of it.

Getting triggered is a normal part of how we're wired. Without the trigger, we wouldn't experience the gift of awareness. It is in that moment of reacting; in the moment of the trigger taking over, that we have an opportunity. In this moment, we can access new self-awareness; the trigger is showing us where we have expectations around a situation. The challenge and opportunity is to move our attention to that awareness and consciously resolve the situation, rather than staying in the hurt and continuing to invest in the story that's playing out in your mind. The gift in our triggers is the moment of awareness when we realise ourselves; we realise a limitation we have, or one of our behavioural patterns.

Emotional triggers are most commonly (though not exclusively) experienced in relation to others. Once you understand this, you are invited to begin interacting and engaging with others in a different manner. Instead of pushing away what triggers you, through the awareness you now have of yourself, you have the ability to shift from blame to personal responsibility, and see triggering situations and interactions as an opportunity for your own growth. Instead of suffering from what triggers you, you are now able to use it as a tool for progression.

Emotion only ever wants to be acknowledged and expressed. It is simply energy.

PHYSIOLOGICAL IMPLICATIONS OF LOVE

Love has a physical impact on our bodies. Think back to your experiences of love. What are some of the physical symptoms?

For example:

- **Elevated heartbeat**

- **Sweating**

- **Breathlessness**

- **Nervousness / excitement**

- **Racing thoughts**

When we fall in love, it's like a homecoming. Love is the light that will be cast over all the parts of you that are in fear, hence why the letting go process is so significant when we fall in love. This process of letting go is as physical as it is emotional. This is because emotion is energy in motion. Emotion is designed to flow through us.

Emotion = **Energy in Motion**

Keeping yourself grounded in love is essential. A favourite quote about this is something a beautiful friend often says to me: "Stand in love, don't fall in love." Often, if we don't feel worthy of love, or don't know how to integrate the power of its presence, we develop a mindset of, "This is too good to be true." This is a belief which results in us pushing love away subconsciously. When we fully open ourselves and surrender to love, we can be transformed by love. It's through this experience we can die and be reborn.

Wisdom is to appreciate love, without ever needing to possess it.

My breakup from my last partner was the beginning of my awakening to love's cycle of life and death. In many ways, my ex had become my muse, our relationship? was my attempt at creating something immortal, from something that was inevitably impermanent. My attempts to capture this love in time was my refusal to accept that we couldn't hold it and own it, forever. I attempted to breathe fuel onto the fire of our love so that it would never extinguish, however, I began to discover that love is much more like water; it will always move. It's not designed to be owned, for owning love is to keep it stagnant. It was through this process of being forced to let go that I really started to understand love and its nature.

When the relationship ended it was as if I had grown to love the storm so deeply that I couldn't handle the haunting stillness that came with absence. I felt paralysed for a long while, as I'd let my head run and run and run and run and run, laying there in an attempt to find answers. I'd let my mind go through its circular process before I eventually realised the letting go process sometimes will lack closure or understanding. The need I had to understand threw me into painful uncertainty. I see now, in hindsight, that letting go is more about celebrating the new, than clinging to the past.

Even pain follows the cycle of life and death, and I've now experienced that the death of pain, will be followed by a deep ecstasy. In pain, if you have evidence to know of its impermanence, it becomes easier to ride the waves. Pain is always impermanent.

I noticed through this process of heartbreak that I still saw her in all things, just as love is in all things, she remained my greatest reference point of love. It showed me that love is so far beyond the physical; physical bounds can't contain or direct love. It exists in a different universe; untamed and uncontrolled. I started to understand something very important.

LETTING GO

Love's design is one of transformation. Love's wiring is programmed to rip you open and give you an opportunity to surrender, to experience a type of death. This is the reason love is so life-giving. If you've experienced a great love (not necessarily just for a person), you will understand the feeling of realising how little control we have over love. Love is so powerful that it is not for us to own, but rather experience. This is a very important distinction. We cannot own the things we love, we can only appreciate them. When my last relationship ended, I began to understand loves not always meant to be soft, it's also designed to challenge us. It's our growth pathway.

To let go of our expectations of how love will play out and allow love to change forms throughout our life is to be free in love.

When I was experiencing this heartbreak, it was as if the universe had fallen away underneath me. Losing her was my greatest test in surrender. I was attached, and with this attachment came the prospect of suffering.

PAIN ASSISTS US TO LEARN PRESENCE

The pain of the heartbreak made me very present, I started operating with a different level of mindfulness. In seeking intimacy, but being too fragile to open my heart to another partner, I began to see the way we can experience intimacy with all things; a conversation with a stranger, riding my bike at night next to the beach, writing in my journal, cooking. All of these things became intimate. I guess I had discovered what people really mean when they say, "It's in the little things." My healing journey was not about radical change, it was about seeing the way love shows up for me in the subtle ways. As the months passed, I started to notice how significant the change in me was, yet how gradually and gently it has happened.

It was through intense heartbreak that I discovered the power of pain, and how it really does work in partnership with love. Without pain, we can't awaken to deeper depths of love. To experience the full power of love, we must be so present; so alive, so activated. Pain reminds us how to feel, and pain teaches us to be present. Pain spurs us to completely let go and surrender control (die), so we can rise as the phoenix from a fire. You can't run away from pain. It was this pain that taught me to love better, simply by understanding love better. Having a deeper sense of compassion and facing my own vulnerabilities meant I wasn't confronted by, or afraid to be with others on their own.

LOVE HELPS PROCESS PAIN, INSTEAD OF AVOIDING IT

It's a special love when you love someone enough to be with them in their pain, instead of attempting to save them from their pain. To save someone from their pain is to rob them of a deeper connection to love. It's an incredible gift to be the one that holds a higher ground and allows the other to process their pain and be a soundboard for their insights and new awareness. To be the one that deeply acknowledges who they are in their entirety; instead of protecting them from their darker experiences.

1. Hold people in their pain, rather than rescuing them. When we are the hero, others become the victim.

2. Endings are always followed by beautiful beginnings.

3. The key is to celebrate the growth, rather than wallow in the loss.

JUDGEMENT KEEPS US IN FEAR

There was a lot of judgement that surrounded my partner and me in the end, with people not understanding where the volatility stemmed from. They couldn't relate to how intense it was to handle such a love and how difficult it sometimes felt to remain rational. What I learnt through this experience was how judgement barricades us from experiencing clarity. To judge someone for their situation is to cut off your ability to support them. Just because we can't understand something, or we haven't yet experienced it ourselves, does not immediately make something wrong or irrelevant. People would tell me, "If it's hurting, it isn't love", whilst failing to understand that love is the torch that shines a light on all of our darkness. I needed to be held in acceptance, and not judgment, so that I could process what I was feeling. I needed a space where I could *fall apart*, to safely go through the process of rebirth. Love highlights the pain we carry- it is our call to growth. Without an adequate understanding of how to confront your darkness, love can become a painful experience as you try and work your way through the mud to get closer to unconditional love.

Love is working to expand and transform you, and pain will surface when we are loved as an opportunity to let go of our pasts, and realise our wholeness.

Love strips us down.

I felt very misguided by my friends at the time, and for the most part, it exacerbated my feelings of confusion and isolation, in a time when I most needed perspective and guidance. Love is found through love; never through separation and fear. It's important for us all to learn to be non-judgemental of one another if we truly want to develop supportive relationships and help each other through difficult times.

This also was something I experienced through anorexia people failed to understand that I was in a love affair with my addiction. It provided me with all the things that others failed to. How could it ever be as simple as 'letting it go', if there was no foreseeable alternative to meet my needs? My needs definitely weren't being met in the office of my therapist, or amongst the community of people who, at the best of times, struggled to relate to the pain I was in; both psychological as well as physical. Love has many faces, and many forms (of course, it's everything). We tend to look through such a tight lens of wrong and right, forgetting that each experience we have is love expressing itself through us. Sure, as we evolve and grow and develop a deeper sense of self-awareness, we will inevitably make choices that create less pain, however, that does not mean that whilst making those, less conscious, choices, we weren't doing the best we could with what we had.

Whilst touring in the van facilitating and speaking around Australia I met many remarkable characters. One, in particular, taught me so much about the strength it takes to truly let go; to be reborn. On our way back up the East Coast we decided to spend part of the school holidays in Sydney. We parked our dusty yellow van out the back of some incredible million dollar apartments in Bondi. It was the perfect place to rejuvenate after months of travelling to new destinations every day and facilitating up to four workshops daily.

During my morning runs in Bondi one woman in particular was extremely noticeable. She seemed to have achieved the corporate dream, sporting her Nike shoes and impeccable yoga attire. I found her poise and manner striking as she walked her dog each morning and afternoon. Once or twice I felt that we locked eyes, but it was hard to be sure through her designer sunglasses. One afternoon I was feeding my dog at the back of the van when she came walking in my direction. My dog, who was never restricted to a leash, bolted up to her Yorkshire. I went to rush and stop Byron but hesitated; knowing that Byron does what she wants. I cringed at this opportune moment to engage in conversation with this lady being tainted by my unruly puppy.

As she approached me she paused and adjusted her sunglasses, "It really is the season for van people, isn't it?"

I laughed before I could censor myself, "Van people?"

"Yeah, the season where all the hippies decide to park their vans all over Bondi."

I took a moment to try and feel out this character. She had a loud presence, for sure, but it wasn't intimidating to me. Saying that I don't think much ever was by this point in my journey. I was feeling very connected and strong in myself.

"I'm just stopping here over the school holidays," I finally replied.

"Please tell me you're older than school age," she went on.

I laughed. "Yeah, I'm on a national tour speaking to schools around Australia exploring? love and connection."

Even through her dark sunglasses, I could see her eyebrows raise with intrigue and surprise.

"The van is definitely the easiest way to get around Australia," I continued, "especially when you're travelling to remote parts of the desert. It's been a crazy adventure..." I rambled on about the adventures I had been on, with little regard for how it was being interpreted or perceived.

After my long tangent she asked, "How do you eat?"

Again, laughing, I explained that I was vegan, so eliminating the need to cook meat made it a lot easier.

She lit up. "Vegan? I just became vegan!"

We had established a point of relatability.

"You should definitely come up to my apartment at some point and I'll make you a nice vegan lunch."

I replied, "Is it suitable for a corporate superstar to entertain a common van person?"

We exchanged numbers.

In the coming days we dined together, and she began opening up to me about her recent realisations about her corporate career. I was enthralled by this new connection, something about her fascinated me. There was an intensity in the way we bonded and the depth of our conversations. Our lunches went on into the evening as I challenged her on philosophy and concepts I could rarely articulate to others. I sensed her spiritual shift, her spirit yearning for something more. Who was I to push what I saw to be the truth? My $3000 van was downstairs as I sat in her marble-floored apartment overlooking Bondi Beach.

There was a fearlessness in my approach at that point in my journey. I had no attachments to anything, so my ability to see clearly came more naturally than it ever had. I saw through fear, straight to the heart of people and situations. It was like a superpower, heightened from the weeks and weeks spent in silence in nature, with no phone or internet. I sensed her sensing this in me, yet being highly confronted by the reality of being seen. After all, I was just a 'van person'. I started to understand the nature of others being mirrors for the self. Irrespective of how we feel others are different to us, each person we cross paths with is mirroring back an aspect of ourselves to us. After all, we are our only reference point. We are only ever looking at a reflection of us. In knowing this, I was more confrontational in my approach with her.

"How can you put assets before your happiness and freedom?" I asked. "How can you see clearly whilst you're so busy protecting the things that are causing your entrapment and unhappiness? We are designed to follow our joy."

I watched her body language, and I could see her resonance with our conversation. Little did either of us know that this was the beginning of a significant and long-term friendship. I became an unlikely confidant in her year-long transition out of a generously paid corporate job in Sydney to becoming a student of wellbeing and hypnotherapy in a beach town in Northern New South Wales. Between catch ups we'd spend most days in communication over the next six months, sharing thoughts and ideas. The distance between age, location and life circumstances dwindled more and more. I watched the shedding of the black suits, the BMW car, the Bondi apartment, and watched the rise of a remarkable practitioner. Through all the letting go, I watched someone who had dedicated fifteen years to a career that she entirely turned her back on, stand up for her happiness.

She became one of my biggest inspirations and a reminder that no matter what or how invested you are in something, it is always okay to let go and it is always okay to prioritise your happiness. I watched many of her struggles and conflicts, resolving the dissonance between her existing identity, and what her heart wanted. I watched this incredible person die and be reborn. I deeply empathised with the pain of letting go of everything, to become something new; to become more of yourself.

It's inevitable that we will endure pain, as discussed earlier, pain is actually a friend in disguise. Pain only becomes an issue when it borders on suffering; on-going, unprocessed pain that holds us in the past. Pain is for progression, not for suffering. In order to truly know this, you must choose to activate yourself in pain and channel that deep insight and perspective into something progressive. We are all alchemists of our own energy; if we choose, we can always shift our focus and use the charge that we experience to create in a different direction.

LOVE AND JEALOUSY

Jealousy is such an overwhelming emotion. It's a human reaction, when we love something, to want to possess it. When we love someone, we become vulnerable to them. There are no guarantees. From so many conversations with clients, I often see shame surrounding feelings of jealousy and insecurity. It's so natural and normal for lovers to trigger these feelings in us. The trick is to deepen your understanding of what the emotion is trying to show you so that you can resolve it without becoming reactive. This desire to 'own' love, rather than allow it to be as it is, without the need to control or change it, can damage and suffocate connection. Jealousy is rooted in the insecurity that there is not enough love to be shared. Love is abundant, and our connection to all people is one of a kind, and the practice of love is honouring that connection whilst allowing the other to be fully themselves without trying to change them.

IT'S A WIN - WIN. ALWAYS.

I remember being ten and turning to my friend before a maths exam and asking if she could help me study because I was struggling. She turned to me and said, "No, because if you do better, I'll do worse". Even then, I marvelled at such flawed logic. Yet, as I grew up, I started to notice how this was the foundation of how many people thought. "You need to be less, so I can be more", "I don't want you to succeed- not that I'll ever say so out loud". Instead, we need to recognise that we are only as strong as our weakest link as a society. For you to 'win', is for me to win. For you to experience love, is for a greater amount of love to exist.

Love is not scarce.

The culture of tall poppy syndrome has conditioned us to believe that kindness, love, success, and goodwill, has a limit. We've become conservative with our love and generosity, out of fear we will 'lose out', without realising that it is within an expression of our own love and generosity that it will be returned to us.

On a greater level, above the perception of competition, the way of the universe is designed, is it's always a win-win. I call it the law of tenfold; whatever I give is returned to me times ten. We must give with the same hand that we wish to receive. What we seek is also seeking us. Love longs for more of itself. This is talked about in the laws of cause and effect. When I remain aware, I always see the demonstration of how my love and generosity has been returned.

When we are scared, we are scared of letting go. We get terrified that our investment in another, or in any sort of endeavour, will be of waste unless we 'keep score.' This is so much so that we miss the beauty and joy that comes from giving without attachment or expectation.

TRANSFORM YOUR PAIN INTO YOUR POTENTIAL

In understanding that emotion only ever needs expression, emotion becomes an activator instead of something that rules us.

Only through complete acceptance, followed by surrender *(a 'death')*, can you transform your pain into your potential.

No one can take away the will inside of you that is crying and craving to turn your pain, your emotional experiences, into your potential. A quote I've always lived by, taken from my deck of Osho Tarot Cards is the following; "What's truly yours can never be taken from you." Yes, this means that people are not yours, things are not yours, jobs are not yours. They are something you are living in relation to. They are something which is giving you a deeper insight into yourself. Your will, your choice, your intelligence, your creativity and your imagination; now, these are things that are truly yours, and sure as hell cannot be taken from you.

I'll offer a very simple example from my own life recently. My laptop is the biggest source of my intellectual property; with years of articles, program drafts, client files, and footage for future documentaries from twenty different countries. About two months ago my charger jack broke. I bought my Apple MacBook into the Genius Bar at Apple to get it fixed, and the man assured me it was a simple process that wouldn't affect the hard drive in any way (as I had not backed my laptop up - *I know, it's crazy how we never think it will happen to us*). A week later, after not hearing from the store, I called to discover my laptop had been sent off and the motherboard had been replaced, meaning three years of my work had been wiped without notification.

It's in moments like this that you realise the choices that we always have. I genuinely know and believe that in every situation of seeming distress and setback, there is immense opportunity for expansion. Only within challenge can we expand ourselves, our thinking, and our capacity to overcome adversity. As trivial as this example is, I use it because I've seen many friends spiral in situations like these, allowing the external circumstance to dictate their mood for days, if not weeks. I received this news a week after I wrote off my new car which I had still not insured. There were many reasons to get down; both from the financial pressure these situations created, as well as the professional impact and emotional loss.

I've been living the practice of love for many years now, and it's when I'm confronted with situations like this that I really understand the benefit. I was, for the most part, unaffected by the circumstances. Yes, there was, of course, an initial emotional reaction that spiked in me upon receiving the news, but I was quite easily able to regulate myself back to a place of neutrality.

I even began to see the gift in the potential situations, thinking that the loss of my work content could inspire me to create newer, fresher content rather than relying on old ideas. It also consolidated that what is mine (my intelligence, my insights, my talent), can never be taken from me, so there is never anything to fear. The practice is to stay calm and not get swept up in the story of disaster. To let go effortlessly, like water, leaves so much space for the new to enter, and the gifts to reveal themselves. To fixate on the situation and its challenges is to leave no focus for the solutions.

Now that you understand the letting go process, you'll understand the freefall is the beautiful opportunity to begin seeing what's next, and what's possible. Just as the phoenix rises from the ashes, as the caterpillar becomes the butterfly, you too will experience a metamorphosis. With the letting go of the old, you will rise with a deep sense of purpose.

CHAPTER 5: PURPOSE

How does love rise up in you?

My purpose was not something that I 'found', it was something at the core- something fundamental to who I am as a person. As purpose will be for you. The more I went through my figurative death, the clearer my purpose became and the more I was able to understand and articulate it. It was the process of undoing, rather than doing, which brought me closer to my core. It was the journey of connecting to my heart, of stepping out of who I thought I was. Purpose is a force much stronger and greater than just you. It's the way you can offer yourself and serve the world beyond you. It's in the interest of all that you discover who you are, so that you can give that as a gift to humanity. When we try and discover our purpose by thinking in terms of "I", it's practically impossible to awaken.

When you change your framing from, "What can I gain?" to "What can I offer? Or 'What can I give?" your life will radically change.

As a young person who was connected to my purpose, I was often confronted by comments like, "You're lucky, you always knew what you wanted to do." This was usually followed by an explanation of how they had never found their purpose. The reality is, most people are misguided when it comes to the nature of purpose.

It's important to understand that **purpose is flexible and responsive.**

I see purpose as an extremely flexible thing. It's responsive when you're genuinely connected to the purpose in your heart, and you don't require a particular set of circumstances in order to be living from it and expressing it.

PURPOSE IS MORE ABOUT KNOWING WHAT YOU _STAND_ FOR.

What do you stand for?

I stand for love.

Coming out of my difficulties as a teenager, and beginning to better understand myself, I awakened to the fact that my sensitivities, insights, compassion and leadership abilities were innate because it was core to my purpose. The deeper I connected to myself and my heart, letting go of the ideas of what I 'should' be, the clearer my purpose become. I started to see that I stood for love. The more I surrendered and accepted this, the more I became a channel and an instrument of content and creative ideas. I began to access a much greater amount of 'flow', and my life became more and more congruent and integrated. I wasn't pushing for what I wanted anymore, I was allowing for what life wanted of me, to express itself through me. I became an instrument for love. That doesn't mean I didn't have to work hard, or take action - rather that my action became inspired and supported. I began to experience expansion.

Through these experiences of surrender and expansion, the nature of purpose became clearer to me, especially in how it relates to love. Love and purpose, much like all other concepts in this book, are in a symbiotic relationship. Expressing your love will be an expression of your purpose; an act of Loving Out Loud. It's the unique way that you can give back to the world because your perspective and way of loving are totally unrepeatable.

So, how do you connect to this inside of you? Take the time to write down the answers to the following questions and really ask yourself;

1. *"What do I love?"*

2. *"When do I feel valuable?"*

3. *"What am I curious about, or drawn towards?"*

PURPOSE REQUIRES SPACE

The more I shed any attachments or ideas I carried around who I should be, the more space I created for my purpose to become clearer and clearer. It left more space for who I actually was to be expressed. Getting to this place required a period of isolation and separation, which we are so often afraid of. In order to gain perspective around my true self, and not the way life had conditioned me, I had to step away from my circles of influence. This is the process you go through during your figurative 'death.' This means separation from the people that hold you within their paradigms and fixed perceptions;

which, due to our need for acceptance, can often stunt growth.

For me this was especially true in the instance of my family as a teenager, yet, it has been something I've experienced during a number of iterations of my life.

As a teenager, there isn't much space to really learn who you are. There are many demands and expectations placed upon teenagers, often reinforced with the attitude 'do it because I told you so.' Even as a child, positive reinforcement of good behaviour is often accompanied with manipulation and blackmail. This is as simple as, 'If you don't do your homework, you won't get to watch television. This reinforcement or blackmail sways us away from our natural instincts of what we're naturally drawn towards, as we fall into the trap of guilt and manipulation. The subtext of this type of learning is, 'We will lose something we love if we don't do something we hate.' This subtext of guilt and manipulation makes us feel like we need to work for love, instead of realising that we are always deserving of it. This frame of thinking is often carried through into our adult lives. And, it makes it difficult for us to believe that we're worthy of following what we love.

For me, stepping away from my family and allowing myself space was fundamental to my evolution and understanding of my purpose. Often when I voiced creative or humanitarian pursuits growing up, it would be met with, "Make sure you have a backup plan," or "With age, you will be less altruistic." This was highly damaging for my spirit during the fragile period of conceptualising and hypothesizing my purpose. I was still in the discovery phase and unable to be entirely committed in my ideas to protect them from opposing thinking. Vulnerability requires enquiry, nurture and objectivity in order to really be supported towards strong and positive outcomes. It was through separation that I made space for new experiences and people who vibrated at the same level as I did, allowing for a deeper and more constructive process of discovery and creation.

During the separation period, it was important for me to practice being alone and learning to back myself- even if it went against other people in my life. I needed to develop the inner strength to follow my heart. It was a challenging experience. My need for validation and acceptance was incredibly strong, yet, I had to become the demonstration of the way I wanted others to treat me.

Within the discomfort of separation, I connected to my purpose. I understood that struggle, discomfort and pain was a component of our experience in order to deepen our capacity to love.

STRUGGLE PUSHES US TOWARDS PURPOSE

As humans, we are always seeking to bring meaning to our pain and our struggles. Having the ability to look back on pain and struggle and know that it wasn't in vain means it makes sense. To make meaning from the times we felt helpless, disempowered and victimised and to justify the times we were the cause of others feeling those things, is to bring peace and resolution to our past.

We seek to weave meaning into the things that have hurt us.

Knowing this, the resistance I experienced in my relationship to my family became the fuel to help strengthen my connection to my purpose. We require the friction in order to generate motivation. We need a why. We need something pushing us away from something, as we are pulled towards something new. It's the frame of relation that we exist in.

My yoga teacher used to say to me, "The object of stretching is pulling," and my personal trainer used to say to me, "Strength is built in resistance." I have always related this back to life, and to the discovery of feelings of deeper purpose. We become more flexible and aligned when we pull our vision (purpose) towards us, and we become stronger when we push against something. When people confront us with judgements that don't resonate with *who we truly are*, we are gifted with a strength to sharpen our connection to our true selves.

Einstein said, *"Great minds will always meet violent opposition."*

The more you stay true to yourself, the more your purpose will reveal itself to you. Purpose requires conviction and it requires an unwavering commitment to self-love. Purpose is the energy that brings our dreams to life.

107

We experience struggle so that we can be pushed towards a purpose, and gain deeper purpose by bringing meaning to that struggle. It's a profoundly beautiful process once you understand the design, and quit allowing pain to defeat you. It's the process of turning pain, fear and struggle into a deeper capacity to love.

PURPOSE IS DEEPENING YOUR CAPACITY TO LOVE

Purpose and meaning are very closely linked. We experience a deep sense of purpose when we find something that is meaningful to us. parenthood, for example. What creates meaning, though? This is a philosophical question that's been pondered over the millennia. Meaning comes when we feel deeply, and when something cultivates and activates emotion in us. The things we love most are the most sentimental to us. It's through love, that we find purpose.

Would it be so radical to suggest that your purpose, here, is to be you? Could awakening your purpose really be that simple? In our world today it seems that one of the leading questions upon introducing ourselves to someone is, "What do you do?" Why are we defined by what it is that we do? Is it not far more important to understand who we are being? For example, if you're an incredibly wealthy CEO, yet who you're 'being' toward your team is arrogant, authoritative, and without integrity, does your material success really outweigh who you are presently being? We need to look at how we provide value to the world as a person. This, in turn, is what motivates us to feel inspired and empowered when we feel we have something of value to offer.

Take some time to reflect. I encourage you to journal around some of your insights leading with the question:

What is the value you bring to the world?

Often we struggle to answer this because we mistake confidence with arrogance, humility with self-love. I invite you to answer these questions by getting out of your own way and owning your value.

DISCOVERING PURPOSE

I'm about to share with you a process I've created to help you discover what your purpose is. Considering one of the premises of this book is that our very nature is love, it's important to understand that your purpose is your unique expression of love. This is what you are here to learn to articulate (which could be through a range of mediums) and actualise, fully. Deepening your capacity to love, through allowing your struggles to push you to create a deeper meaning, and allowing love to pull you towards your vision, will ultimately act as the formula to help you awaken to your purpose. The deeper your capacity to love (out loud), the more you're able to express your purpose.

Let's break this down.

This process is centred around one question:

How does love RISE UP in you?

How do you know when you're in love? What is the feeling that rises up in you? How do you express your love?

Do you know you're in love when you start to become fiercely protective of someone or something? Do you know you're in love when you begin strongly considering someone in your thoughts and decisions? Do you know you're in love when you begin wanting to offer someone comfort and when you want to nurture them? Do you know you're in love because you feel your heart come alive inside your chest? There are psychological, emotional and physical components to our experience of love, completely individual to each person. It's your job to familiarise yourself with these 'symptoms of love' in order to begin moving closer towards love.

We all have different experiences of how the love inside of us expresses itself; of how we love out loud. When you have conscious awareness of how love rises up in you, you have a compass to understand what choices and opportunities in life align most deeply to your expression of love, and the people in your life who bring out and cultivate the love inside of you. Quite often, when we haven't familiarised ourselves with our version of love, it's difficult to align our choices to love. Once you know how to do this, you have the ability to align your choices and your direction to the limitless nature of love, and the whole universe will begin supporting you in the actualisation process.

There are a few ways to become familiar with how love rises up in you.

The Symptoms of Love

1. Love's physical presence
2. Love's emotional expression
3. Love's psychological condition

Let's explore these further.

Firstly,

1.   What is love's physical presence in you?

Every emotion has a physical implication. Love has one of the most profound effects on our physiology - think of the sudden strength a mother demonstrates if their child is in danger. Familiarising yourself with how love impacts you physically is a quick and effective way to check in with yourself. Often our minds try and hijack our feelings and 'convince' us we feel something, when in fact our bodies know differently.

This is called The Felt Sense. The Felt Sense is specifically defined as, 'the embodiment' (bringing awareness inside the body) of one's ever-changing sensory/energetic/emotional landscape. The Felt Sense moves our focus from actions and things happening outside of us; in the world, to focussing on our present, internal experience. It's extremely powerful to become aware of this, particularly in regard to love.

For me physically, I know I'm experiencing love when I sense total expansion in my chest, an elevated heart rate, a feeling of light energy pulsing up and down my spine, and a feeling of total elation. Maybe you experience something like this when a cute guy or girl chucks you a 'like' on Instagram (let's hope this isn't your highest example). Love is that rush of energy that occurs when something lights you up and activates you. It's important to note, however, that these initial physical feelings of love aren't necessarily what continues as that love becomes more deeply integrated. As love strengthens, and settles, and is no longer a novelty, we become more grounded in our physical experience of love. For me, once love has become more deeply integrated, I feel it as a physical strength. And, although this is a powerful presence, it has a sense of humility and gentleness. A deep physical feeling of having nothing to prove, nothing to justify – and specifically nothing to DO; deep 'knowingness.' This is much like a gentle smile from the inside my being. It's significantly different to the feeling of lust, and the rushing sensations that come over me when I'm experiencing temptation. It took much discernment to not be fooled by the feelings of temptation, and learn to follow the path of love, a much fuller and deeper feeling.

A really good process to begin tapping into this is to do what's called a stream of consciousness writing. Begin by getting a piece of paper and pen, and write the sentence *"In my body, the sensations I feel when I'm experiencing immense love are...."* and continue to write for five minutes without breaking pen from paper. If you feel blocked during the process, continue to write whatever comes to your mind even if you feel it's nonsensical or irrelevant. The idea is that the pen can't stop moving. This process is about connecting you to your subconscious, and therefore bringing about new awareness.

Once you have completed this process, read back through what you've written and reflect, or journal, on your insights. What are the sensations you feel physically when you're experiencing love? Take the time to become deeply familiar with this.

If you still feel unclear, you can use this process to drop deeper into your awareness. This is a process I frequently use to check in with myself.

1. *Close your eyes, and draw your conscious awareness to your breath. Relax your body, through bringing your awareness and focus to your breathing.*

2. *Relax the mind, and observe any judgements that arise for you... As they do, know it's normal, and gently guide your focus back to your breathing.*

3. *Once the body and mind are relaxed, visualise a time you were experiencing immense love - and notice where your awareness immediately goes.*

4. *Wherever you find your love expresses itself, connected deeply to this. This is your life-force, your power.*

5. *Physically familiarise yourself with this feeling.*

6. *Give this feeling a colour, a texture, a sound; really connect and associate your physical senses to this feeling, so that you can more easily access it and come back to it when you feel lost, or stuck.*

7. *Honour this deeply.*

8. *Open your eyes, concluding the process.*

Once you understand the physical feeling of love with you, it becomes much easier to access when you feel disconnected or feel as though you're lacking meaning and purpose. If you can bring this feeling into the different experiences, environments and relationships in your life, you're on purpose and aligned to love.

2. What is loves emotional expression in you?

How does love express itself emotionally through you? This will be multi-faceted, however, use these questions to gain clarity for yourself.

1. What emotions do you feel when you're experiencing love? (Both for something and someone; e.g. excitement, curiosity, determination).

2. What emotions do you feel when someone you love does something that hurts you? (Sadness, mistrust, anger).

3. What emotions do you feel when something you love breaks, fails or doesn't work? (Failure, withdrawal, upset).

4. What do you feel when something you love is succeeding? (Happiness, optimism, joy).

Asking yourself these questions provides you with a deeper awareness to identify these emotions as they rise in you, so you're not letting love pass you by, but rather you're in conscious awareness as to how love expresses itself through you. By understanding the ways love rises up in you emotionally, you're also able to extract the unique way you have to express your purpose.

To provide an example, a few of the extremely strong emotions I feel with love are a fiery sense of courage, a strong feeling of protectiveness, and a deep, unquenchable curiosity / intrigue. When I start feeling these emotions towards a person, or a project, I'm now quick to identify that it's my love expressing itself towards them or it. Whilst I felt disengaged and under-stimulated in my university lecturers, I had a deep feeling of fire inside of me when I'd daydream about following my dreams. My body was very clear about what my true path was. We've learnt to shut down our intuition so much, and have allowed the truth to be twisted and manipulated by justification in the mind, that we often don't notice these signs. The more you trust your body, the easier it will become to identify and place these feelings. The more you follow the feelings you wish you feel, the more you will begin to see the world reflecting what it is you desire... If you create from an emotional place of struggle, hardship or negativity. consistently, it becomes harder to let go of what you've built in order to start again from the right energetic and emotional foundation.

TRUST YOUR FEELINGS

During the first ever presentation I gave, I was so nervous that my hands were shaking as they gripped the piece of paper that had my speech written on it. I was unsure if following what I knew was my passion and purpose. The vulnerability associated with being a beginner at something was something I had always struggled with. It was hard to differentiate between my fears and my true feelings. It was a massive shift for me to understand that when I experienced that vulnerability towards something, it was actually an indication that I loved it and that it was important to me. I was choked up as I had 400 students looking back at me. I could feel their eyes looking at me, even though my eyes were fixed on my piece of paper.

This was the first time I had shared my story publicly. I could feel the shame and fear run through my body, and the imposter in my mind shouting that I wasn't good enough. Normally I had enough self-control to cold push those thoughts to the back of my mind, but now it was at the forefront of my thinking. What was I doing? Who was I to believe I could normalize this conversation? It was at this point I reminded myself that most people's greatest fear, after death, was public speaking. It was a terrible thing to remind myself of, but this final burst of that fear propelled me to do something magical. I lay my piece of paper down on the floor, and through the vulnerability of looking my audience in the eyes, I sunk straight into my heart. I expressed what the process of moving through mental illness was like for me. I let them in. I let them know why it was difficult for me to share it with them. I made it clear I wanted to share my truth and help them understand and feel that if they had ever experienced similar experiences or emotions, that they weren't the only ones, and that it was okay.

My courage rose up in me and took over from my fears and insecurities. I found a point of such deep connection within that vulnerability, and was guided to a place of overwhelming love for myself, the audience, and the opportunity to share that time and space with them. It was the first time I had ever experienced a standing ovation. No part of that experience made me feel egoic, or like I was all of a sudden, the world's greatest speaker - it was me finally giving myself the permission to be seen as imperfect and to have that be acknowledged. Permission to realise that love moves people because it celebrates the imperfections and the messiness of it all, and finally, to experience what it was like to be received, fully, as myself; just as I was. It was a deeply humbling experience. It was in this moment of intense vulnerability and permission that I realised what love truly feels like emotionally- the courage, the appreciation, the acceptance, and the gratitude.

This experience helped me distinguish emotions that were driven by vanity, or lust, from emotions that were truly anchored in love.

3. What is loves psychological effect on you?

What happens to your thinking when you discover love? Do you start to become more limitless in your thinking? Do you begin to see beyond someone's flaws? Does your mind open to different possibilities? Do you naturally start to become more imaginative and creative?

LOVE AND INCENTIVE

Love has this illusive superpower. It seems to make the impossible, possible. As it changes your state (in particular, your thinking), love often makes people think more divergently and creatively, and there's an explanation for this. We become more divergent and creative when the incentive is strong enough. For example, if you are lost in the wild, you may have never hunted an animal, or tracked food before, however, the prospect of starving to death would be enough incentive for you to attempt these things. When you love something enough, the incentive of love overpowers any excuses, barriers or limitations you may have put in your way. For example, a guy at work may have been wanting to ask his colleague out for many months. She approaches him on their lunch break one day and asks if he would like to get a drink with her that evening. Without hesitation, he accepts the invitation irrespective of the fact he knows he has other plans. After she walks away, he too begins reflecting on how strapped for cash he is, and how much he wants to be able to shout her drinks the whole evening.

He confronts two obstacles; cancelling his plans, and finding the cash to take her on a date. If it were someone he wasn't as drawn to (or in a state of love for), these obstacles would generally be enough of a reason to decline and perhaps reschedule. The power in love is the sudden ability to be resourceful and creative in solving problems, and boldly asking for what it is you're actually wanting. The incentive becomes too big to say no to, regardless of the obstacles.

When you relate this to life, it's important to ask yourself if your motivation is coming from love; because if the answer is yes, you will develop superhuman powers in overcoming limitations to achieve the outcomes you're wanting in your life. If you're in an intimate but loveless relationship, when challenges arise the motivation to do the work required to overcome those obstacles will seem too great, and the cost of the effort won't seem worth the prospective outcomes. This is the same in your work; if the outcome does not seem worth the effort of what's required to reach it, then there's a good chance you aren't experiencing enough love towards the project.

Once you have a frame to identify how you experience love, you can begin designing a life that you love all aspects of, broadening your perspective of love further than just relationships. Look to your whole life and ask if your life is bringing out the 'symptoms' of love in you.

To follow love is to follow the path of expansion.

It's important to understand, also, that your experience of love may change as you mature and evolve, and only through careful observation and presence will you be able to identify how love is rising in you and how love is showing up for you. Often what we 'think' love should be, is different from the way how love is trying to manifest itself for us. We need to overcome our judgements of how we believe love should be, so we can become aware of what it actually is. It's good to reflect on how you learnt love as a child, and if you still want this to be the way you seek love. Often our experiences of love as children can have a negative impact on our ability to embrace love as it shows up for us. For example, your parents may have expressed their love to you through material means, providing you with gifts and assets to show their affection, so this may be what you learnt love was. But perhaps it isn't actually the means in which you genuinely feel fulfilled in love. We get stuck in what's familiar to us, rather than what our hearts truly crave.

Through surrendering your expectations of what love is, you allow love to blow you away and surprise you with its magical nature. Often those we love most were the least expected and showed up at the most unsuspecting times. Love's nature is designed to break our expectations of it; to surprise us. Love has a potent, undisputable presence in us- irrespective of how it looks.

LOVE CREATES PSYCHOLOGICAL FLEXIBILITY

As you align with things you love, you will notice that you won't be as narrow in your thinking. You will be able to be adaptive and responsive because you're more committed to the feeling of love and the vision rather than the specific way of getting there. Approaching life with this amount of agility is an extremely valuable asset that most successful entrepreneurs have. It is a state of divergence, where your mind is looking at solving problems in a multitude of different ways.

Neurologically, to be in a fear state is to be operating from the back part of the brain; the reptilian brain, which is over two million years old. When you're operating from this part of the mind, your thinking is extremely limited - it is a survival technique. This is specifically designed to narrow your thinking so that you can focus on responding to the threat. It is so overpowering that you will even, in extreme cases, have narrowed vision (designed as a survival strategy to either attack or run away from the threat as quickly as possible). In this state there is a significant amount of adrenaline pumping through the body, and there is no space to be creative or divergent in your thinking.

In my workshops, I see many symptoms and examples of people operating from a fear-state, while completely unconscious of this fact. During a sacred circle, that I facilitated recently, there was one woman in particular who showed multiple signs of operating from a fear state. The group was connecting deeply, sharing stories and allowing the power of the group to support them through transformations. (The more I develop as a facilitator the more my approach becomes hands-off, because having a very soft control over the group allows space for them to facilitate and mirror each other). I observed this woman as she refused to share her perspective or input. I sensed that the fear of vulnerability and judgment were overpowering her capacity to be held by the love in the group. It's in these instances that I'm very aware of not jumping in to save someone from their discomfort, because it is within that discomfort that they will grow. I asked her a direct, soft question, and held the silence for as long as it took for her to share. It was interesting to feel the tension in the room rise as people's irritation and uncomfortability consumed the space. We're so often frightened by silence because of the nakedness it brings up. It was within this silence that this woman was able to have a significant breakthrough, have the courage to share, and move past the fear into a deeper space of love.

She became a return participant after this experience, and watching her ability to speak to a group and her receptivity to love grow has been a fascinating thing to observe. I am now able to identify the ways she has stepped into a loving mindset, and approaches her life's challenges with a completely altered perspective. It's a beautiful journey to witness.

There are distinct ways to identify the ways love and fear play out in our thinking. Here are some key elements to help you decipher where your thoughts are coming from:

LOVE-BASED THINKING	FEAR-BASED THINKING
Expansive	Restrictive
Inclusive	Reactive
Divergent	Impulsive
Creative	Judgemental
Solution-focused	Narrow
Compassionate	Selfish
Altruistic	Limited in perspective

Now that you're familiar with purpose and how it rises in you, it's a natural by-product of this process that you will activate a deeper sense of creativity. Purpose requires creativity in order to actualise itself. Let's explore this.

(LOL) Love **OUT LOUD**

How will you birth your purpose into the world?

Creativity: so many people have varied views around what creativity is, and how to access it. Here, I'll be sharing with you a framework that has allowed me to not only understand my creative power, but to measure it, enhance it, and most importantly, expand it.

Something I often hear people say is, "I'm not creative." It's a ludicrous thing to think about yourself. Our *essence* is creative and our soul *longs* to express itself. As you venture through death (Chapter 4) and the deep process of letting go, you are resurrected with a deeper sense of purpose. Now you are opened up to the inspirations and insights that spark your creativity and are able to experience the motivation that has the power to bring your dreams to life in order to make something real from the calling in your heart.

When I first felt called to begin writing this book, and more broadly creating this body of work, it felt so immense and conceptual it could have easily made me feel debilitated. When you think about a concept like *love*... How do you quantify something so intangible? I had my work cut out for me.

Growing up I always felt a deep craving to express myself, to become articulate enough in an art to bring my imagination to life. I think this same craving is at the centre of all of us. Yet, there's a distance to travel before we reach a point of articulation or mastery. Few of us will experience being born prolific; a writer must work at their ability to tell stories and explain concepts, a guitarist must go through years of calluses and hours of frustration before they become fluent with the strings, a dancer must fall and ache before they make it look easy.

Although we are all creative, few dedicate themselves to becoming masterful. This is as true in art as it is in life. What we need is a frame to measure and express our creative spirit. To progress. There's no shame in being a beginner - after all, a marathon is ran one step at a time.

Creativity Requires the Ability to Quantify

In the beginning of writing this book I needed to breakdown what my objectives were and what the elements of love were that I deemed important to explain. I had to think about the frame that was going to consolidate and carry my message. When you're creating, it's necessary to understand where you are going. It can seem like a contradictory process as creativity is about going into the liminal, absurd, and the abstract. But, to create usefully we require structure.

What are some of the things you are trying to create in your life at the moment?

Answer these questions:

1. *What is your starting point?*

2. *What resources, skills or intelligence do you need?*

3. *What are the outcomes you want?*

4. *What steps need to be taken in order to achieve the desired outcome? (The more quantifiable the better).*

FAILURE STIMULATES CREATIVITY

We need to cut the stigma. Failure is a misunderstood friend.

Before you throw yourself into the process of creating, please understand that failure is a crucial part of the creative process. It allows us to learn, to experiment, and is required if you want to become masterful in your art and life. Creativity is birthed in discomfort- it forces us to be creative. We learn so much more from our failures than we do from our successes (much of the time). When you find your own path, and discover something that really inspires you, you are assisted to reframe failure as learning, and problems as challenges. This is still an unfamiliar concept for society as a whole, so it's possible you will initially experience a sense of isolation when you begin to think differently and reframe your life. The thing is, when you start to become a conscious creator, your path will be innately different to others. It will be the path less travelled, as it is the path designed for you. You are the one here to build and follow it. When I became clear of my path, many people in my world thought I had lost my mind. But, I knew this was a common experience for those who decide to chase their dreams, so I deconstructed what sanity, insanity, creativity and normality were. After all, why are we so bound by these constructs?

SANITY

Sanity: "The ability to think and behave in a normal or rational manner."

Normal: "Conforming to a standard; usual, typical or expected."

The very definition of sanity insinuates that in order to be sane, it requires you to conform to the majority, and act in an expected way.

Creativity: "The use of imagination or original ideas to create something; inventiveness."

Innovative: "Introducing new ideas; original and creative in thinking."
We live in a world that supposedly promotes conformity and is against 'insanity', yet highly values creativity and innovation. This is a dichotomy many people feel trapped in. They don't want to experience a separation from the group, for there is a fundamental human need to feel accepted and a sense of belonging, yet they also strive for personal expression, tapping into their creative genius (genius, in its Latin origins meaning genuine).
Once you let go of attachments to 'sanity' (normality and conformity) you will be in a free-fall with love. Similar to the notion of 'falling in love', you're opening yourself up fully to embrace the potency of life and its pure creative energy. It is then that you can become an instrument of it. Through this sense of openness, you will begin experiencing your true potential, creative gifts, and alignment.
You can access this in every moment. Every moment you can die and be reborn, every moment you can love to the fullest expression of yourself. You can sacrifice all that holds you back; your pride, your stubbornness, ego, identity, and let love continually transform you into more and more of yourself. This is loving out loud.

Love's got your back.

Love wants you, it's seeking you to be reborn in the face and image of itself. Love only ever seeks itself; so, to align to it, is to know love will always have your back and support you to grow alongside it. This is how I interpret the religious connotation of God loving all of his children and always seeking a personal relationship with his children. He is you. You are love. Love is you.

JUDGMENT IS A KILLER OF CREATIVITY

Our fear of failure often manifests as the judgment (and insecurity) we have around our self-expression. I've found that judgment is one of the biggest killers of creativity. Having said this, it's very important when we're in a process of creation to practice discernment.

It's okay to say NO.

There's a distinction that must be made between judgement and discernment. Discernment allows us to shift through noise and become focused, whereas judgment stunts our curiosity, which is crucial for creativity. We need to become fascinated by something in order to experience awe and inspiration.

Human nature has always fascinated me - I've described that curiosity as insatiable. My art form (writing and storytelling) has become the lens that I've held up against reality. It's the filter that lets me make sense of things. When first writing this book I became insatiably curious, I became the investigator.

Step 1: Asking The Right Questions

The first step in this process was asking myself the right questions. What is love? What does it mean to people? How do we seek it? What are the elements of it? How is it expressed? What is its anatomy? By asking the right questions you begin to focus in on what's relevant. You become discerning. You begin to see something unique. This process allows you to become more and more clear in your own perception. When I started to break love down into the components I started to see a pattern. I began to understand that there is a fundamental foundation in which love is experienced which was also mirrored in my own journey.

A good way to simplify your answers is to ask: *"How would you explain it to a seven-year-old?"*

Simplicity is key. When you truly understand something, you're able to explain it simply and concisely. Simplicity speaks to clarity. Turning your purpose into action and expressing it to the world requires creative focus.

Before we get stuck into creativity itself, let's have a quick look at some barriers to creativity.
The largest? Judgement.

Step 2: Shifting Your Judgments

FEAR MANIFESTS AS JUDGEMENT

The first step in changing your relationship with fear is to understand how it may currently be manifesting within your reality.
It's important to note that fear will manifest itself as judgement, and whilst we're in a state of judgement of either ourselves, or others, we are blocked from actually seeing what it is we need to confront. It's also important to highlight that not all judgments will manifest themselves as a negative. For example, when you say to yourself, "That person is so much more talented than I ever could be," you are observing another's talent, but you're also undermining your own ability to recognise in them what resides in you. Our observations always come from our own perception. What we notice in others is always a mirror of ourselves. This is the same when others' judge us; it is a projection of their relationship and awareness to and of themselves.
There are simple practices that can help you overcome these barriers. All they require is the ability to observe your thoughts. Once you have an added layer of awareness in your thinking, you're able to notice and become

more aware of the judgements that cross through your mind. With this awareness comes the opportunity to override your judgments, and analyse the gift in them (which is fear highlighting itself to you). This then gives you the opportunity to work through, and confront the fear, allowing you to expand your perception of the world, and move closer to love.

FEAR - PAIN - GROWTH ZONE - LOVE

There's a process to understanding how to move from fear to love, and yes, there will be times it feels painful and uncomfortable. I like to see these as 'growing pains', just as a child suffers from physical growing pains as their body grows, our consciousness will also grow through pain. Challenging a judgement that you hold is an opportunity to expand your perception and horizons of love and acceptance more than you thought possible. Through this process, there may be an initial discomfort, as you push yourself into the unfamiliar.

THE SYMPTOMS OF FEAR

1. We judge what we are yet to accept in ourselves.

2. We reject what we are unwilling to confront.

3. We deny, or ignore, what's in front of us.

It's very important to understand that this is only ever about you. This is never about the situation, or the other person. If we judge, deny or reject another for their differences, this is a direct reflection upon ourselves and generally because it speaks to an insecurity within us.

A key, pivotal shift in your thinking will help you immediately approach these situations with more love, and provide an immediate opportunity for your own expansion.

This shift is in knowing that love is multidimensional. It is pure consciousness, therefore, can be found in anything and everything.

I discovered this when I realised I had fallen in love with my work. It gave me a way of creating that gave me a deep feeling of self-expression. I was in a love affair, and what it provoked in me was no different to the romances I had experienced with others. My relationship with my work was literally a love story and a two-way relationship as it taught me as much as I informed it. It was a symbiotic relationship (as all love-based relationships are). I wanted to be romantic with my work, take my time with it and experience it deeply. Over time, the feeling of urgency settled, and was replaced with excitement, willingness, openness and inspiration.

I found myself in love. Literally. Time became irrelevant. The challenges were reframed into surmountable opportunity, a way to grow myself through playing and loving out loud. I had no hang ups, only an acceptance that it was it for me. No matter what angle I looked at, it seemed perfect. The details no longer seemed to matter and I stopped being caught in the 'how' or the logistics, I was fully invested into the why.

Why it was important to me was all that mattered.

WHY, LOVE?

Love has a tendency to lift you above logic, and transplant you straight into the why. It gives you purpose, and meaning, and previously perceived barriers and limitations tend to fall away with ease (like magic), as synchronicity (discussed earlier in the book) takes over and guides you into a more seamless flow of creativity. This is because your focus has changed. You are no longer focusing on the barriers; but rather the life force that comes with love. It's naturally life giving. You become receptive and open, rather than defensive and closed.

WHAT YOU FEAR IS YOUR OPPORTUNITY FOR EXPANSION

Generally, we judge what we don't understand or what is different to us, just as we fear the 'unknown' or 'unfamiliar.' The brain is designed to stop us from experiencing the unfamiliar, as once upon a time, the unfamiliar may have meant danger. Or in extreme cases, death. It is the unfamiliar, however, where we grow and gain deeper insight; where we move closer to oneness, and therefore closer to love.

Fear can become the ultimate instigator of creative inspiration when we know how to use it as fuel. Fear marks the danger and the mystery that makes art and creativity so delicious.

If you rewind the clock to the 1950's, women still didn't have the vote, and homosexuals were imprisoned. As we've evolved and these things have become not only socially accepted, but socially normalised, it can be concluded that these differences actually held the space for our expansion as a civilisation. If we look at this on a micro (or individual) level, it is no different. The situations that evoke fear in us are the same situations that we often judge, reject or deny, are actually holding the space for us to grow. Once we normalise what we once saw as different, we have expanded our perspective and our sphere of acceptance, and in doing so have deepened our capacity to love.

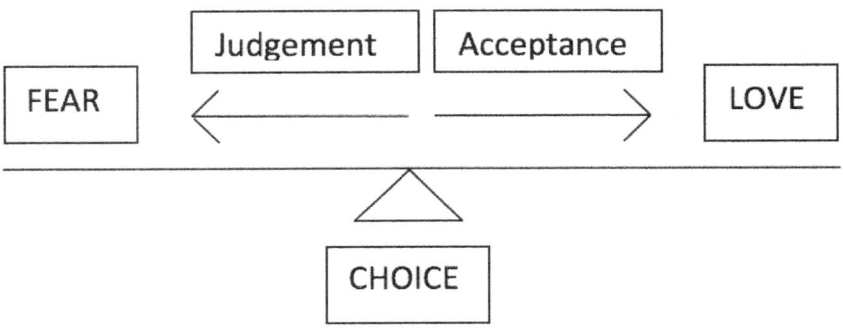

If you look back through your own life, you will easily find examples of this. Often, we evolve our realm of acceptance and familiarity unconsciously. We are not always conscious of how it's happened naturally and organically over time.

Think back to your first day at a new job. Think about the degree of judgment you may have felt around your own abilities before you were exposed enough times to the certain tasks and responsibilities. Over time did you develop a fluency that meant you no longer felt insecure about your abilities?

Think back to when you first met a friend, or a partner, and the aspects of that person that were still unfamiliar to you. No doubt over time your acceptance and love for that person grew as they normalised themselves in your world.

Think back to the way you used to think in high school; the defining ways or relation (whether that be fashion, looks, sports etc.), and how that's evolved into your adulthood.

Fear became the pathway for your creative expansion.

You can begin to bring conscious awareness to this process, which will help you become mindful of your judgements day-to-day, and provide you with an opportunity to grow at a much faster rate.

The more you work through your judgements, the more receptive and open you will become to new experiences, and the more deeply you will be able to engage in these experiences.

ON THE OTHER SIDE OF JUDGMENT IS CURIOSITY

Creativity flourishes through curiosity. The less judgement that plagues your mind, the more space there is for enquiry and curiosity, which is the prime state for learning. Through acceptance we begin to engage and interact with our realities differently; acceptance allows us to have freedom. Without the burden of a judgemental mind, we eliminate comparison and stop investing our attention and energy into our opinions of wrong and right, acceptable and unacceptable, and therefore we awaken to a reality where everything is as it is. We can relate in wholeness to things. We can experience ourselves in a broader way.

What is the distance between your fear and your love?

THE DISTANCE OF LOVE, IS DETERMINED BY THE DEPTH OF FEAR

Love and fear exist in polarity with one another. What this means is that regardless of whether or not you've had an experience of unconditional love, you can gauge the distance between you and love by understanding the depth of fear you experience.

For example:

The polarities of fear/love or love/hate rely on each other for our experience of them.

If your work has asked you to give a presentation in front of colleagues and you feel your fear is at a 9/10 at the thought of public speaking, this indicates that the opportunity of growth is also at 90%.

However, if you had to chat with your best friend and give the same information, your fear would probably be at a 1/10. Why? Because there's already so much love established in your relationship; this becomes a safe space, and therefore the fear is non-existent. We fear what we're unsure of; the unknown; the spaces and situations where we aren't yet sure we're accepted and loved. These are our opportunities to grow our self-love; and once we grow into a deeper degree of self-love, this will manifest itself externally and you will find that confidence is reflected back to you.

We experience things in contrast because without resistance and contrast it's impossible to truly experience things at all. An analogy I love to use;

> When you're riding a bike and you ride your bike in first gear, it's quite easy to ride (there's no resistance for your legs to push past), however, what you'll eventually find is that it's difficult to go faster in a lower gear. However, if you shift your bike into 6th gear, although this is more difficult initially, once you push through the initial resistance, you're able to travel at a much faster speed.

What this shows us is that the resistance we experience (in this case, our emotional/psychological resistance rather than the physical resistance in the bike analogy) is actually our greatest (and extremely necessary) opportunity to grow and move further towards our potential (love). On the other side of a growth opportunity lies expansion and only progression can come from these experiences.

You have so much creative potential inside of you: unlimited, in fact. It's time to learn how to actualise it.

To harness your own creativity, it's crucial to have a starting point and an endpoint. Many creative people struggle to articulate their vision, often stuck in their ideas and imagination. Without a framework in which to think about creativity, it's hard to express it.

To understand that you are a creative being is to understand your power in creating the life you desire. To harness your creativity is to actualise your purpose.

Here is the frame that allows me to understand my creative expression and enhance my creativity abilities:

THE TENSION BETWEEN LOVE AND FEAR CULTIVATES PROFOUND CREATIVITY.

When contemplating whether or not to begin a creative pursuit, what is the biggest deterrent? Fear. Fear of starting, fear of the hard work, fear of inability or lack of talent, fear of others' opinion.

The list goes on.

And what is the thing that allows you to conceptualise your creative ideas, and execute them? Love! Love for your art, love for the dream, love for the opportunity, love for yourself and your freedom of expression, love for the value your endeavours will bring to the world.

The way I see it is this:

Our capacity to actualise our creativity is determined by:

The distance between the amount of love you hold, and the fear that consumes you.

We need to understand where our love ends, and fear begins, in order to access more and more of our creative potential. When you can overcome fear, and strengthen the horizons in which it impacts your thinking, emotions and behaviours; you will have more creative abilities and freedom to build the life, projects, business, relationships of your dreams.

Once you understand this, your ability to consciously create your experience will wildly transform.

There are two ways of looking at your fear;

1. The barrier that prevents you from expressing your love (loving OUT LOUD).

2. The tension that slingshots you towards your vision.

For the most part, people's view of their creativity is clouded by the former. They are consumed by their fear. The best artists and most successful minds have mastered the latter. They understand that between love and fear lies a tension that becomes creative fuel.

"The deeper the sorrow carves into your being, the more joy you can contain." - Kahlil Gibran

CREATIVITY AND DESTRUCTION ARE SYMBIOTIC

"The Tortured Artist" is a historical cliché. I want to highlight that there is actually a tangible reason why artists are more affected by destructive behaviours and emotional lows. Being an artist, or being creative in nature (which we all are, some are just more in touch), requires a deep level of sensitivity. There is a flow to creativity that even nature follows. This sensitivity in artists allows them to use their fears and emotional lows as fuel to create. This doesn't mean it's essential for an artist to be tortured in order to create, but rather that a creator can rise up and create from any experience. With their sensitivity also comes a remarkable antifragility. This is not dissimilar to what can be witnessed in nature.

It was in Costa Rica when I noticed something that altered the perspective of my own creative nature. I was trekking through the forest; admiring the incredible, natural environment, and revelling in my own insignificance next to the mighty force of Mother Nature. I had always admired nature and perceived it as egoless and fearless. As I was contemplating this, I walked past two trees and noticed that the vines of one had grown around the other. I asked my guide what this was and why this happened. He explained that often in nature, even trees fight for survival. In this instance one tree was 'strangling' the other, competing for sunlight. He pointed out another species of tree that was shedding its skin to ensure termites couldn't penetrate it, and another that was growing extra roots so it could move geographically to access more light. I was stopped in my tracks.

"You mean even trees fight for survival?"

He chuckled, "Fear is an instinct throughout all of nature."

It was then that I awakened to the truth of fear. Fear is our sense of self. It's our ability to differentiate ourselves from everything else. It is our ego. It is our capacity to have a unique perspective, and unique ability to be creative.

Destruction is a natural part of our world, and thus our own creativity. In nature, this is called entropy, which is the breakdown of something so that it may be revitalised.

Entropy is defined as a *"lack of order or predictability, gradual decline into disorder."*

We can take this understanding and use it to empower us, rather than destroy us. Through accepting that there is a natural flow to our creative process (and more broadly our lives) when destruction happens, we can acknowledge and recognise this as an evolutionary trigger that is preparing us for a new chapter in our lives.

This first requires you to change your relationship with fear, and thus your relationship with destruction; using it for creative power, rather than being stuck in cycles of destructive behaviour patterns, or 'addiction.' When you look at the true meaning of addiction is defined as a 'tendency or inclination.' Most behavioural patterns are arguably addictions- it's just that some are healthier than others. When you become conscious of these patterns, you have the power to transcend and change them. The natural order of our life is cyclic, and all parts of the process must be appreciated and leveraged for our creativity and growth.

Step 3: Let Appreciation Lead To Inspired Action

When we can look at all experiences as an opportunity to create, we are given an immense gift: the gift of appreciation. We can appreciate all things that we encounter as we realise it's through the diversity of these experiences that we can find inspiration. When we can completely appreciate something, and not judge it or try to change what has happened, we can experience what it's like to truly be inspired.

APPRECIATION LEADS TO INSPIRATION

When we are in a state of appreciation, we cease needing to change things and instead see these experiences as an opportunity to create from them. Appreciation gives us access to an incredible state of awe, which is a powerful catalyst for inspiration. When we are trying to control things, and not taking a step back to simply appreciate things as they are, it is difficult to feel inspired. Inspiration happens when we stop trying. Just like Isaac Newton had his epiphany when the apple fell from the tree after he had sat quietly for hours and hours on end, we too are in the best condition to experience inspiration when we have surrendered our expectations of someone, or of a situation. We can't control what happens to us, but we can damn well choose what we're going to do with it.

You will become unstoppable when you allow yourself to take a step back from judgment, or what's happened to you, and replace it with the perspective of appreciation, and begin allowing your past experiences to become the fuel that propels you to create. When you allow yourself to be inspired, you will feel an impulse to create. It won't feel like a chore or a task, but rather an instinct, to create. By appreciating things, you are left only with the gifts.

When you appreciate things with loving eyes, and a loving perspective, you can create diamonds from the pressure of pain. Conversely, if we spend too long appreciating low vibrational emotions and experiences, we risk becoming destructive. When we glorify pain, anguish, or hate, we are being inspired to create from these emotions, rather than love and compassion.

We choose the frame in which we process experiences.

We are the meaning makers of our experiences, we choose what things mean to us.

So:

1. *How do you frame things?*

2. *What is the creative fuel that drives how you construct your reality and life?*

3. *What do you appreciate, and how does that inspire you?*

PART THREE

INTRODUCTION

Congratulations on finishing Part Two. Part Two is the more chaotic and confrontational part of the whole transformation process. As you move from 'the separation' (Part 1), and then 'break down' (Part 2), you move from the chrysalis to become the butterfly. Through the process of transformation, the caterpillar moves into the cocoon where a complete breakdown happens *(a challenge phase)*, where a death occurs and a transformation is beginning, so that the caterpillar may become the incredible butterfly. The phoenix burns in the fire, so it can rise from the ashes.

I honour your journey.

From here, your reintegration begins; the process of acknowledging your journey, and learning to fly. Through the previous growth, your insights have strengthened and deepened, and the person you were before you began this journey has been replaced with a version of you that has more clarity and awareness.

Due to the nature of our culture we often struggle to deeply acknowledge another's transformation processes, as it holds up a confronting and powerful mirror back to us; inviting us to look at the areas of our own lives we have been avoiding or dismissing as part of our evolution.

This means that, at this point, in your journey, you may feel a dissonance between you and those around you.

I must highlight to you that this is a normal thing to be experiencing.

In facilitation, I call this process "the entering of liminal space"- the space in between. It's the space of separating yourself from your known, but not yet being the recreated version of yourself. It's the exploratory phase. During your reintegration from liminality, it's important to be extremely careful and gentle with yourself, explicitly taking time to deeply acknowledge the process that has occurred. Doing this assists you in being able to look forward with the right frame of mind, and take the conscious steps to fully honour the process of your evolution.

At this point in your process don't allow others to make you doubt yourself. It is here you can be asking yourself questions like:

"Who is aligning to me at this point in my journey?"

"Who are the ones strong enough to acknowledge my process, instead of fearing it?"

"With these new insights and this new awareness, what is shifting and changing in my life?"

"What am I wanting to move towards?"

"How am I wanting to offer the new version of myself to the world?"

The next few chapters are going to guide you through a very solid, and extremely crucial, acknowledgement and reintegration process so that you can completely own who you are becoming.

(LOL) Love **OUT LOUD**

CHAPTER 7: ACKNOWLEDGMENT

How can you alchemise your pain into beauty?

As I discussed in the prologue, acknowledgement has a profound ability to transform pain into remarkable beauty. I shared the story of my school principal, who in my time of crisis, stopped to be truly present with me and directly acknowledged the pain I was experiencing. It was as a result of this acknowledgement that I was able to begin my healing journey. It was here that I realised that when we avoid or deflect, our choices and circumstances, we fail to take responsibility for our lives. Without responsibility *(the ability to respond)* we aren't able to make changes to our path.

Yes, acknowledgment is confrontational.

Only a crazy person would look at their shit dead in the eye and say, "I choose to love myself and forgive myself, and more importantly, face myself."

Why would you willingly put yourself into this excruciating pain?

There are very, very good reasons why.

YOUR LIFE UNFOLDS IN PROPORTION TO YOUR COURAGE.

The more courageously you acknowledge yourself - baggage included, the bigger and more expansive your life will become. Acknowledgement is courageous- it is not for the faint-hearted. The times in my own journey where I have courageously stood up to the truth, confronted something that scared me, have always given me the richest reward.

In mid-2016, on a 42-degree day in New York City, I was walking through the streets of Brooklyn thinking about the previous evening. The city that never sleeps was, ironically, inspiring me to look at the times in my life where I had been asleep; the elements of my past that I hadn't yet acknowledged or resolved. It was one of the first moments during this trip that I had really stopped to be quiet and acknowledge what had actually been going on for me. I had been grappling with the impending decision that I needed to make upon arriving home. I realised that I had been avoiding thinking about it so that I didn't have to take responsibility for myself. When we acknowledge something, we're then confronted with a responsibility to it. I specifically remember asking myself whether or not I was having a quarter life crisis; that point between childhood and adulthood where you realise all your expectations of life were far more fantastical than realistic. When you begin realising that you don't "grow out" of your problems, you realise that age holds no weight in maturity, unless you actively participate in your own development.

I picked up my phone and typed into Google, "Is a quarter-life crisis a real thing?" I clicked on an article reading the first sentence that stated, "The chances are you're having a quarter-life crisis if you're googling it."

The following morning I decided to go to the gym. Firstly, it was air-conditioned, but more importantly, I was riding that initial buzz of motivation that comes after crippling life realisations. As I stood on the treadmill my mind was spiralling in anxiety. I was fighting to not return to a place of victimhood in my thinking. I went to reach for my water bottle and, as I did, I caught a glimpse in the mirror. My attention was snagged by a man walking behind me. He had the most gorgeous, clean-cut face, carrying himself with this incredible sense of pride and confidence. He had an immaculate posture and an incredible physique. It took a few moments before I scanned down his body to see his two prosthetic legs, and I was hit in the gut. *"Wow,"* I thought, *"that's courage."* The courage of not running away from, or becoming the victim of your circumstances, instead deeply acknowledging your past, and from that acknowledgement gaining the strength to become better and stronger than you've ever been. This man in the gym, irrespective of the difficulty of his past, had used it to propel himself to a new degree of strength and growth. He demonstrated courage in circumstances that others may have crumbled. Acknowledging your mistakes, your downfalls, the unfortunate events that feel like they've tainted or taken from you, gives you the power to turn our pains into our biggest breakthroughs and strengths.

Acknowledgement takes courage, and in turn, will vastly increase your capacity to create a meaningful life. In a world where self-medication is a social norm, it's difficult to even grasp what acknowledgement looks and feels like. I want to support you in understanding what acknowledgement is, and how you can use it to alchemise your pain into beauty.

During the darkest and most uncertain times in my life, it's been incredibly painful and overwhelming to acknowledge what was truly present for me. It's much easier to ignore or deny what's going on because once feelings and challenges are acknowledged, there is a responsibility to feel and process what's there. Denial can often seem like the easy way out. A saying that encapsulates this well is: "Easy choices, hard life. Hard choices, easy life."

The power of acknowledgement is transformation. Once something is acknowledged, it begins to shift through the awareness that has been brought to it. This is a skill that we need to learn, as it is often something that we did not (necessarily) experience in our childhoods.

As children, if we were exposed to "sweeping problems under the rug," or if we weren't taught effective communication tools in order to properly acknowledge and resolve problems, then it becomes apparent that we haven't learnt the right tools, or frameworks to resolve our challenges or pain. This can then develop into feelings of being unseen or lacking the sensitivity we needed to feel understood and safe. This will continue to play out during our adulthood unless explicitly addressed.

How may this manifest in our behaviours as adults?

ACKNOWLEDGEMENT AND DEFENCE

If we haven't experienced what it means to be seen and acknowledged as children, then we often compensate for this in the way that we interact with the world as adults. If we experienced rejection or feelings of being misunderstood, it's possible that we've centred our belief systems around this.

Through the lens of a child, you see the world through innocent eyes. You can feel when something doesn't feel right, or good, but you have no capacity to rationally deconstruct situations, which leaves you impressionable and vulnerable to your family, specifically. Basic examples like having a door shut on you, without a significant adult realising, and you create a belief system like "I am not wanted," or "I am not loveable". Some of the most common subconscious belief systems I see in clients are;

For example:

"There are parts of me is not loveable."

"There is something fundamentally wrong with me."

"I need to hide certain parts of myself in order to be accepted."

If we then experience acknowledgement in our adult lives, it may go against the deeply ingrained belief systems we have created for ourselves. If this is the case, we may react to acknowledgement with deflection or defensiveness.

I see this very often in my work. Simple acts of acknowledgement evoke a deep discomfort in people, and they react either through deflection; exhibited through laughing, using humour, looking away, changing the subject, directly shutting it down, or, also, through defensiveness such as not being able to accept it as genuine, searching for an agenda behind the act of acknowledgement.

It can sometimes be painful to be seen. Yet, this is so crucial if we want to grow into our potential. Often our light, and our power frightens us because it challenges the limited belief systems we have about ourselves; which is the reason it is often emotionally experienced as discomfort, irritation, or perhaps even anger.

ACKNOWLEDGEMENT AND YOUR REALITY

Your mind is the sole creator of your experience. What you are acknowledging or not acknowledging is profoundly important when it comes to the makeup of your reality. We often believe that we need to focus on the problems in order to fix them. This couldn't be further from the truth. We just need to acknowledge problems in order to refocus our attention on a solution - or to use this acknowledgment as fuel to focus our attention on something we would prefer to be experiencing.

In meditation this is called *becoming the observer.* To become the observer of your experience is to have the control and ability to shift your focus at will. Learning the nature of acknowledgement helps us become the observer.

As a society, acknowledgement is foreign to us. This is because we have grown up in a world which, in many ways, has taught us to run away from ourselves and our problems. As a result, we have shied away from our potential, and sold the story to settle for mediocrity, because let's be real, that's all that is actually achievable.

During childhood, as we learn many of these messages, our greatness and the uniqueness of our perception is failed because we aren't acknowledged. During this time, we are graded against archaic and cookie cutter systems that value the stale recollection of facts, numbers, and letters.

It is only through the honest acknowledgement of our individuality that we then develop the self-belief and grit to really pursue the life we were always designed to lead.

We have been so under-acknowledged. In fact, for most of us, we struggle to receive a compliment. Acknowledgement is not a nicety, it is a profound, raw and powerful way to create transformation and growth; propelling us towards our potential.

During a workshop I ran in the middle of 2016, a man stepped forward and shared the details about an up and coming adventure he had planned; designed to push him to his limits. He was going to hike Mount Kilimanjaro.

When I facilitate, I use the energetics of a space to guide transformation and insight. Space to a facilitator is like paint to an artist. As he explained some of his anxieties, I stepped back; enabling the group to gain a deeper and deeper understanding into the hike.

I then asked the man to select two people from the group- one person to represent to stand at one end of the room and represent him now, and the other to stand at the opposite end and represent him as he finished the trek. The space in between the two versions of the man represented the journey, creates a scale (and a frame) in which to experience emotion (energy in motion). Understanding that the unconscious mind is all-knowing, means that it already knows the emotional process between where we are and where we wish to be. However, often this is clouded by anxiety. As I walked this man through his journey, he talked through his process; from what it would feel like to leave his partner at the airport, to standing at the bottom of the base, all of the cold nights sleeping on the mountain, all the way through to the feeling of elation experienced watching the sunrise from the top.

As he moved through this process, it became clear he was extremely emotionally invested. And, as a result, so was the group. So much so, everyone present stood and clapped at the end of the process. The other workshop participants were so inspired that they felt compelled to offer him support and feedback, acknowledging what they saw in him; *commitment, trust, faith, execution, will, determination.* I stood back and observed the effect acknowledgement had on this man. His stature and energy had completely changed. He had, in 30 minutes, transformed himself from extreme anxiety, and hesitancy, to confidence and clarity. His level of articulation had changed, alongside his body language and interactions.

By consciously opening the space in the room, this man was able to confront his unconscious, unacknowledged self and feelings. If not for opportunities and spaces like this, we get stuck within the moments we haven't fully resolved within ourselves.

This man's experience of sharing demonstrated to everyone in the room the power that acknowledgement has on our ability to view situations with greater clarity and refined execution. To be fully seen is to be held. Being seen provides us with an opportunity to go through a process safely, and allows us to be vulnerable enough to gain clarity around our situations.

Whereas, a lack of acknowledgement; a space so many are stuck in, creates huge challenges throughout the rest of our lives.

ACKNOWLEDGEMENT AND RESPONSIBILITY

Acknowledgement is one of the most profound superpowers we have. Having our truth acknowledged by another person is to be fully seen. Therefore, making us accountable for our own potential. Throughout history, different tribes and societies have known this and centred their sacred ceremonies and rituals around acknowledgement. They had the wisdom to understand that via acknowledgement, members of the community would be compelled to step up to their responsibilities.

People will grow to the degree in which you expect them to. If you expect the worst of someone, there's a strong chance that the person will only ever grow to meet your low expectations. If you set the bar low for the academic performance of a young person, there will be limited access to any inspiration and motivation to try and exceed that expectation (except the rare few who have a very active, innate sense of their own potential). For most of us, we become the product of our environment, and the people (and their expectations) closest to us.

What we acknowledge in each other is what will begin to define us. There is a marked difference between acknowledging one's true nature and their unlimited potential, and, for example, acknowledging someone's physical appearance.

True acknowledgement helps us distinguish the profane from the profound; the mundane from the sacred. Being in a process of acknowledgement is deeply transformative because to acknowledge something is to fully embrace it.

Acknowledgement: "to accept or admit the existence, or truth, of *(object)*."

As discussed, if we haven't experienced a deep sense of acknowledgement in our childhoods, then we experience specific shifts in our belief systems as adults. One common recoil is that we are then of the belief (much of the time) that we can only find self-acknowledgement, through seeking others' approval. What is the easiest way to get someone's approval? It's often achieved by being like them; reflecting the parts of themselves that they love and accept, and through not confronting them and risking rejection. This makes it difficult for us to ever experience the authentic type of acknowledgement necessary to progress forward in life, and specifically to progress from pain.

In order to begin receiving acknowledgment from life, we must first learn to acknowledge ourselves.

1. Take time every day to connect to the deepest part of your nature; the love inside of you. This might be via reflection, meditation or journaling.

2. Begin to acknowledge others in the same way you wish to be acknowledged. Yes, this will feel uncomfortable. The more you practice it, the easier it will become.

3. Receive from the world. Instead of deflecting a compliment given to you by someone, lean into the compliment by thanking the person, and giving yourself permission to receive it.

The more we practise acknowledgement, the more we unlock and uncover our unconscious and unknown beliefs and ideas about ourselves. To receive acknowledgement from others often challenges our own views about ourselves.

We then need to utilise this as an opportunity to shift and reform the beliefs we have; aligning our focus to the strengths and value others see.

In practising self-acknowledgement, we begin to deeply honour and acknowledge what arises within ourselves by choosing to love these things, instead of dismissing, running away, or judging them, we are giving ourselves an opportunity to re-frame, to rewrite and reconfigure our limitations. The only way to begin processing, letting go of, and changing negative emotions and beliefs is to acknowledge them and allow your acknowledgement to change your relationship with them. By fearing what we feel, we allow our feelings to have power over us. We often run away from what scares us; as we judge what scares us. Through acknowledgement we can shift from fear and judgement to a loving and centred relationship with ourselves, becoming an observer rather than a victim of our experience. This reignites our awareness of choice, and power to refocus in a different direction.

ACKNOWLEDGEMENT GENERATES CONNECTION

During my recovery from anorexia, my doctor made a deal with me. I desperately wanted to live in Oyonnax, a little French town outside Lyon, on a school exchange. The thought of not being well enough to go killed me, so my doctor said that if I managed to hit a certain weight target in time, I was allowed to go on the trip. This goal became a major motivator for me- and, I achieved the target.

At six in the evening, whilst in Oyonnax, my host mother would call the family to dinner. We'd sit around the dinner table, and even though I wasn't fluent in French, we'd do our best to communicate about our day, as well as having philosophical conversations and broader discussions about politics and our views. We used a lot of body language. I'd laugh and connect with them; genuinely feeling a sense of community. Most nights, it would blow me away that by the time we'd leave the table I would realise that we had been sitting around for 4 - 5 hours. The focus of the evening was never about the food specifically, but rather the opportunity, through ritual, for connection. My French host family had a very different relationship to food and wine in comparison to my upbringing in Australia. Instead, breaking bread was an opportunity to bring people together. This was a passion that was contagious. Food no longer was about weight or restriction, it was the focus of celebration and abundance. Food became synonymous with joy.

I became fascinated by the power this (very simple) experience had in transforming my state, and more deeply, my relationship with my (eating) disorder.

Being in this community was an awakening experience for me, specifically around understanding acknowledgement.

Being heard + being seen + being valued = the feeling of acknowledgement = a feeling of connection and love.

Staying with this family, I found the deepest sense of acknowledgement and acceptance that I had felt to date. Especially given my circumstances back home. During this time I reflected on why that was, and realised there were several elements:

1. They saw me, and not the illness. *I wasn't defined by a set identity.*

2. They involved ritual in their every day. *This consciously and deliberately created the space for acknowledgement to exist.*

THE MUNDANE AND THE SACRED

Acknowledgement is sacred. There's a breakdown of ritual in our society directly correlated to the lack of sacred time and space we experience. This disconnect results in a lack of genuine acknowledgement it. The reality is that deep acknowledgement requires presence, attention and intention.

Once upon a time, we had a strong connection to ritual. Traditionally, the process of acknowledgement happened through ritual; it was a process of acknowledgement; of deep receiving for the individual. The individual would experience the process of surrendering and receiving the truth. The truth has nothing to do and nothing to prove - there's no trying or searching when it comes to the truth. The truth always remains, irrespective of our momentary ability to face it. The gift in this, however, is when we are finally ready to face this truth and acknowledge ourselves, we find ourselves in the right condition to evolve into the next iteration of our expansion.

Through the old rituals, we understood the importance of giving thanks to the sun, and the moon, and the land and the rains. We understood the cycles of the day and the year. We understood the celebration that came with new life and the deep spiritual understanding of death. We understood the power of a having a tribe, and our connection to one another. These were crucial distinctions from the day to day duties of hunting and gathering. We understood that to eat the flesh of an animal, was at the sacrifice of its life. There was an honour and deep acknowledgement that came with everyday experiences alongside that.

In a society where our access to acknowledgement (or an attempt to find it) is being driven by comparing ourselves to others on social media, it is no wonder so many of us fail to transcend our pain and turn it into something beautiful. Where in today's world do we experience the sacred? It's important to understand the difference between the ordinary and the sacred because it is hard to understand, or even feel, what it is to be in a state of deep acknowledgement (acceptance of truth) if we are forever running away from ourselves, our mistakes, our pain, past relationships, and past trauma. Being stuck in the mundane, and not utilizing it to bring us closer to the sacred, makes it impossible to acknowledge, not only ourselves but other people in our lives. The reason acknowledgement is sacred, and I'd even go as far to say holy, is because of the deep reverence and sincerity that is in true acknowledgement. When we sit in a space of truth - even when it's confronting, uncomfortable or painful, we access the doorway to liberation, growth, expansion and most importantly, beauty.

DISPOSABILITY VS ACKNOWLEDGMENT

Today's meat comes from a supermarket, and relationships from a pseudo-connection from Tinder. Today's entertainment is delivered, on demand, by the click of our Netflix button, and food to our door without ever having to converse with another human being. Today's self-worth can be derived from the number of 'likes' on an Instagram photo- never mind the fact that these many of these people would never answer your call in a crisis. Today, we go to bed with our back to our partner, numbing the pain of our days with the all too familiar glow of our iPhones. Today's 'busy' means numbing the pain of each day with a five o'clock wine- or six.

Where's the line between our mundane, and our sacred?

Our current reality means that, in having easy clickable access; the next high can be accessed with something as simple as a swipe right. What we might not be cognisant of is that through these every day on demand experiences, we are building a belief system founded on the learnt practice that possessions, moments and people are disposable. This, in fact, takes us further and further away from the deeper acknowledgement of our experiences and each other that is required to be truly present.

There's the unspoken expectation that our behaviour, and our pursuit of acknowledgement, will deliver a tangible satisfaction to our deep craving. We expect this, without questioning the way in which we attempt to find it. How can we really expect a person on Tinder to see us, in the profound way our soul craves, when the medium is based on making connection convenient? It's only through focused intent and mindfulness that we will be able to both give and receive the acknowledgement we crave.

THE BEAUTY IN THE MUNDANE

It's important to note that the appreciation of our mundane experiences is also important, and can only be experienced in contrast to sacred and profound experiences.

There's a crucial beauty in the mundane; seeing the beauty in the simple acts of day-to-day life. The mundane is the necessary tasks that bring meaning and contrast to that of the sacred. Think of the process of survival; the hunting for food, the collecting of wood for the fire. Today, in a world of convenience, discomfort has become foreign. Mundane tasks are generally done for us by technology or convenient services.

In a modern-day context, where we are given the comfortability of our modern-day life, we aren't learning to acknowledge the work required to actualise great outcomes. We live in a society where being significant and ambitious is glorified, yet our culture conditions us to become the opposite. The cultural narrative we're often told is one of safety and conservative decision making- to not upset the status quo with different or 'left field' ideas. We've learnt to value safety above risk-taking; vulnerability over self-expression. We've learnt to expect that we can be the most beautiful, the most popular, and the most successful instantaneously. We are trying to access these sacred experiences without the knowledge and willingness to participate in the journey, or the process. We're terrified of being beginners, or students because we're terrified of being seen as not good enough or failing. Without acknowledging the process and the work required, we limit our own potential. There is beauty in the journey, and in the mundane tasks- they teach us humility and allow us to become masters of our own perspective, through bringing meaning and contrast to what is sacred to us.

ACKNOWLEDGEMENT AND VALIDATION

I want to explain an irony to you. Our failure to confront things, and embrace acknowledgement, is the very thing that fuels our need for validation. By not acknowledging ourselves, we seek validation through others. Our heart craves a deeper connection, yet we spend so much energy searching outside of ourselves looking to find what we already intuitively know. Your heart knows the solution to this search for external validation, and has a magical ability to alchemise your pain and bring a deeper meaning to your past, and more importantly a purpose for your future. We need to stop doing. We need to stop looking into the void of superficiality, and we need to start deeply acknowledging ourselves, first and foremost, which will then have a natural flow-on effect to others

We can only give to the degree we are capable of receiving.

I've often found that clients I've worked with have experienced incredible disempowerment because they feel that others use them, yet they are the ones enabling others to do so. We must learn to bring the responsibility back to ourselves and be the example of how we wish to be treated. When we shift responsibility, we are placing an unspoken expectation on the other person that they will be the one creating feelings of worthiness, or wanted-ness.

Until we can acknowledge the deeper needs that drive behaviour, and more importantly, what drives blame, no attempt at seeking superficial acknowledgement will be of any benefit.

HONOUR

Once you begin to get comfortable with acknowledgement, you will begin to carry a new sense of honour within you. You will feel a deeper sense of self-respect, and others will most likely begin to feel magnetised towards you. People sense, even if it's not conscious, those who can truly see them, and not deflect or run away from meaningful and real connection. You'll notice that you start to 'skip the small talk' and crave deeper conversations. Your capacity to experience compassion will deepen. Offering respect to others will, in turn, increase the way others respect you.

ACKNOWLEDGEMENT AND TRUST

Through the practice of acknowledgement, your capacity to trust yourself will strengthen dramatically. Trust is crucial when it comes to the most significant things in your life. We require trust in ourselves first, before we have the ability to trust others. Without trust in self, we doubt our judgements in other's character, and more generally, our day to day choices. Trust is a complex concept; what makes us trust some people, and distrust others? What is the difference between someone who is completely able to back themselves, and those that get trapped in doubt and hesitation?

Trust requires us to truly acknowledge ourselves.

I feel trust is broken down into these key areas;

Boundaries and respect + reliability.

We first need to have a clear sense of what our boundaries are in order to state them to others and develop a feeling of trust through then having these boundaries respected. Acknowledgment is such a crucial component of being able to identify and communicate what our boundaries are. Unless we can properly acknowledge ourselves, including our sensitivities and needs in relation to others, we cannot identify what our boundaries are. When we avoid looking at our own needs, wants and desires, we lack the frame required to build trust. This is also true when it comes to our ability to respect ourselves and be consistent and congruent with our words and actions. Our ability to demonstrate reliability through staying true to our word is what our reputation ultimately relies on. Trust is built over time, and never through one single act of greatness. Only through repeated demonstrations can we build trust.

Trust is like a building.

With every act of deep acknowledgement, we accumulate more and more materials which build a stronger structure. Each relationship has its own building, including our relationship with ourselves. The building of these towers goes both ways; when we acknowledge others and when we feel deeply acknowledged by others. The feeling of being acknowledged, which we

155

experience as a feeling of being seen, creates a feeling of kinship and loyalty. For this reason, it is damaging when a connection is seen as disposable. In these modern frames of relationship, often we aren't given the right conditions for our trust to grow. When we immediately approach connection with the mindset that it's disposable, we aren't entering the relationship with the intent, respect and communication required to develop trust.

Exercise

1. *Think of a time when you felt a great sense of trust in yourself. What were you acknowledging in yourself?*

2. *Think of a time when you felt a great deal of trust in another. What did you feel they were acknowledging in you?*

Having the courage to completely acknowledge yourself will give you the strength and trust to walk the journey to your potential. You will provide yourself with the self-assurance necessary to stand strong in your growth and transformation and to avoid the risk of falling back into old behavioural patterns or ways of life. Once you have complete trust in yourself, and your perspective on life, you transcend the risks of being influenced or misled by others. Here you will become the master of yourself, and of your unique way of Loving Out Loud.

CHAPTER 8: GRATITUDE

How can love become your ultimate perspective?

Gratitude has had a lot of marketing over time. We learn the importance of manners, and to be grateful for what we have. We learn to eat all the food on our plate because some people in some parts of the world don't have the same luxury. However, I feel that in this constant use and promotion of gratitude, we've lost our genuine connection to how gratitude actually feels- and the purpose it has in our evolution. When we are forced to practice something, quite often our emotional association with it is negative. It is with this negative association that we miss the gifts in the practice of gratitude.

Gratitude is not a chore. Gratitude is the complete knowing that life is always working for us. It's the foundation of growth, and the protection of all the gifts we have in this present moment.

We humans are funny, we usually don't understand what something means to us until we've had the contrasting experience of what it's like to live without it. We grow familiar with things, which often comes with a sense of expectation, entitlement or complacency.

On day three of my most recent flu, my fever was rising and my throat was burning. I had such a longing and gratitude for my health. In the days following the flu fading, I told myself, "I will never take my health for granted again." Yet, a week later that remark was forgotten as the feeling of health returned to normal.

A big part of creating a gratitude practice for yourself is the understanding that gratitude is about honouring what has become normalised in your life, so that it may be sustained.

Gratitude is one of the most powerful practices we can adopt because gratitude allows us to nurture and grow what we already have, as well as transmute destructive and painful experiences into progressive learning opportunities. Gratitude is the deep knowing that life is on your side. To honour the gifts in each experience is to become indestructible. It's not enough to practice gratitude when things are going right; the true practice of gratitude is most relevant in the moments it seems the hardest.

FEAR AND ANGER CANNOT EXIST IN THE SAME SPACE AS GRATITUDE

Gratitude cannot exist simultaneously with fear and anger. Compassion is birthed from gratitude. To practice gratitude is to see beyond the fear and the anger and to offer purpose and meaning. Fear and anger are two of the most sabotaging states to reside in. Firstly, as has been discussed throughout the book, fear is the separator between us and all things. When we are in fear we are disconnected, and thus cannot access our true potential, and innate nature. Anger is a secondary emotion, meaning that it can only be experienced as a mask of a deeper emotional state. For example, if anger is rising up in you as a result of being hurt by someone you love, this is happening because anger is a mobiliser, it's designed to help you progress radically forward through hurt, suffering, pain, or frustration. Failing to understand this, however, can mean getting stuck in anger, which is heavy on the nervous system and can wreak havoc in someone's life via erratic and unregulated behaviour. Anger needs to be expressed in order for us to land in gratitude for the experiences that have been challenging us and causing us pain.

In 2015 I was working on one of many contracts in Central Queensland. It was an extremely remote, drought affected community that had recently lost fifty percent of its population due to the devastation the drought had created. Families were forced to move elsewhere- even though they had been farming there for generations. Sadly, there are particularly high suicide rates in these areas, due to the shame many of the farmers experienced in not being able to provide for their families and cattle.

I always experienced a feeling of deep reminiscence when I was out West. In particular, as I watched the sunsets over the dry, cracked terrain. That harsh landscape used to well me with emotion and acted as a powerful reminder that we all go through periods of drought in our lives; periods where we're not sure when the rain is going to come next. It's only through the drought that we're gifted the opportunity of a breakthrough - gratitude. We need the resistance in order to create enough pressure for us to rise above it. It's in the drought that we learn.

As I greeted the six-young people I was going to be working with on that initial week-long intensive out west, I remembered that these young people were all battling droughts of their own. There are multiple ways to approach a drought. We can get angry; *"Why! Why is this happening to me?"* Blame often spurs anger, which can often seem extremely justified. Another, more productive approach, is to trust and understand that we are part of a much broader, intelligent design. Rain will always follow the heat. Pain will always be followed by joy.

One of the six-young people was harbouring large amounts of anger. It was a challenging case, particularly because she didn't want to be there. I was the easiest target for her anger. Of course, I was the one there to push the triggers and have the uncomfortable conversations. My objective for

(LOL) Love OUT LOUD

the project was to bring these young people a deeper understanding of themselves, their psychology, and emotional awareness.

On day two I decided to open the space with a story of my own significant rite of passage. I described what it was like to feel misunderstood and ostracised through my teenage years. I described what it felt like to not have support when I needed it most.

Throughout this narrative, I watched the way she became to become restless; fidgeting and desperately trying to avoid being present in the space. This girl had spent the whole day withdrawn, not contributing. She wore a beanie and entirely black attire in 40-degree heat, constantly looking down. I continued, explaining the feelings of victimization, and my inability to see the gifts, until much later in hindsight. I explained that unless we become aware of how we're making our choices, and how our experiences have and will continue to shape us, we don't have control of how we're being initiated into the new chapters of our life.

Suddenly, as I opened the conversation up for the group to share what some of their rites of passages and defining moments had been, she lit up with an intense passion. Her engagement was still charged with anger and laced with pain, but nonetheless, the conversation had activated her.

"We do not have the correct rites of passage in our community. We're not supported to think big, or dream or love ourselves. You're an outsider if you ever try and say something positive," she declared.

Anger was her ammunition; fuel for her potential. I realised, very deeply, the power of anger when it is used to mobilize us. Yet, just like this girl, so many of us remain in silence. In silence, we can allow our anger to birth us into a deeper understanding. By acknowledging this anger, and expressing ourselves, we will ultimately land in a deep gratitude for our experiences, as they have grown and strengthened us.

We spent the next five days strategizing how these young adults could be voices of change in their community, championing these ideas and concepts and changing their community's culture. In the concluding reflections, this young girl confessed something so powerful, it defined the way I understand gratitude. She shared, *"After being heard this week, and understanding how my experiences have gifted me with a deeper insight into myself, and strengthened my compassion for others, I feel grateful for all the experiences that have brought me to this moment, that have made me who I am today."*

160

Residing in gratitude is to land in the deeper wisdom inside of you. Gratitude can be cultivated, like all emotions. Very often we wait to feel life moving, in order to move; whereas a champion will adopt the mindset understanding that we can cultivate feeling, via movement. To practice and focus on gratitude is to become stronger and stronger at embodying it, and it will eventually be the automatic place you land. Repetition trains the brain to regulate itself in specific ways.

INTEGRITY IS TO LOVE THOSE WHO HATE YOU

It sounds intense, I know. To love those who hate you, or to love those who seem to be the supporters or creators of disharmony or pain, seems counterintuitive, however, we all know the saying, "An eye for an eye, leaves the whole world blind."

To align ourselves to those with hateful hearts is to be no different to them.

It is in these moments where the practice of gratitude and love is most important.

This understanding has been crucial to the development of my leadership skills. There have been many iterations of practising and strengthening my love to bridge the distance created by others hate or judgement of me. I've constantly practised stepping back from taking things personally, and instead learning to understand that often we cannot choose the character we play in someone else's reality. We have no control over how someone else perceives us, and sometimes by honouring ourselves, others may not immediately understand or accept our choices. I've always struggled to be the villain in someone else's reality, so until I became comfortable at this, I was always controlled by other's expectations of me. Firstly, I needed to understand that everyone's feelings are valid even if they hold a very different perspective to mine. In their reality, they have a reason for feeling the way they do. Our capacity to land in gratitude in these moments is to see their

161

behaviour as an opportunity to strengthen and broaden our own love.

To understand that the people who have caused us pain are in pain themselves requires deep understanding and a superhero amount of compassion. It's important to note, however, that this is not only a gift to them; it's a gift to ourselves. To be hateful towards another is to drink poison. We are the ones harbouring the negative and harmful emotions.

The hack in transmuting hateful or negative feelings towards situations or others is gratitude. Train your mind and your heart to rest in the knowledge that there's a gift in all experiences, even when we are struggling to identify them. In these moments, a useful tactic is to go back to basics - what are the very basic things you are grateful for?

For example:

"WOW! I have breath. With my breath, I generate the ability to be alive!"

"I have emotions that allow me to feel and more deeply understand who I am and what is meaningful to me."

"The pain I feel reminds me that I have sensitivity and the ability to care."

"I have food, and shelter and water."

"I know all experiences are impermanent."

It almost seems too simple, yet throughout history gratitude and humility has been marked by every spiritual philosopher, teacher and greater leader as the most powerful form of alchemy. It immediately shifts your state and allows you to reframe your perspective, turning everything you experience into gold.

GRATITUDE IS THE BRIDGE TO MOTIVATION

Often people believe that their lack of discipline is the reason for their shortcomings. I strongly argue that discipline is not your problem.

You already do what you know you have to do; you go work, even if you hate your job. Why?

1. It pays your rent and you **need** somewhere to live.

2. It pays for your grocery bill and you **need** to eat.

3. It affords you the **freedom** to go out on the weekend.

4. It allows you to travel.

You do what you have to do because there's a motivation for doing it. It's basic human psychology; we do not do anything without a motivation for doing it. Even if the motivation isn't consciously known to us.

We procrastinate because the thing we are procrastinating about doing is not important enough to us. We do not feel a sense of gratitude towards it, or there is simply no 'need'. Gratitude is a brilliant hack to understand what's important to you. When you visualise your dream and step into it as if it had already become actualised, do you fill up with a sense of gratitude? If the answer's yes, you have found motivation. When you discover this, you can move from a mindset of survival; "I have to do this", to a mindset of motivation; "I want to do this!"

Discipline will follow motivation.

We don't need to live our dreams, though we can be highly motivated to achieve and actualise them. Gratitude is an extremely key player in this equation. Without a sense of gratitude at the prospect of what you're wanting for yourself, mixed in with gratitude for what you currently have, it's hard to

163

progress.

When I was rehabilitating my body, I found myself switching from the victim mindset of my past to becoming grateful that I even had a body that could be trained into strength again; gratitude gave me the power, strength and antifragility I needed to actualise my desired reality of health and strength. During my illness, the majority of my awareness was placed on the negative symptoms I was experiencing. Due to the fact the eating disorder had such a strong grip on me and often left me feeling out of control (by the end of the illness), I felt like a victim. Through the victimisation of myself, it was impossible to redirect my focus onto points of gratitude and love, making it extremely difficult to shift my energetic state. This made recovery impossible as I was perpetuating the negativity. As I started to move through my recovery, my awareness started to move to the things I was grateful for. Instead of focusing on the things I hated about my body, I started to become aware of how amazing my body was and how blessed I was to be able-bodied. This realignment of my focus meant I was constantly feeding my body with gratitude and love, which made the healing journey much faster and more effective.

BEING GRATEFUL FOR DIFFERENCE

One thing I've really discovered through my journey is how our differences are, in fact, our biggest gift. Often our differences are etched into us as a result of having had challenges that shape us to think and act differently. However, differences are also often just our natural quirks; the cause for us to feel alienated or separated from others. Often, we allow these quirks to be the source of disempowerment. We could, however, choose to understand that, instead, they are the source of our power, and should actually be celebrated. Often, we find it difficult to embrace the thing that seemingly 'separates' us because they set us apart from those around us, but this is a big part of Loving Out Loud; to both accept and love our quirks, as well as celebrate the quirks in others.

"To be yourself in a world that is constantly trying to make

you something else is the greatest accomplishment." - *Ralph Emerson*

When you have something about you that is different from the 'norm', or what's currently 'socially accepted', you are a space holder for our expansion as society and more broadly humanity.

By highlighting the difference, you become a beacon of awareness. Through awareness and the power to capture people's attention, you provide a profound gift to others, inviting them to expand their current paradigm and way of thinking. Understanding that you are uniquely beautiful, uniquely skilled and perfect as you are, ought to not be a 'long journey.' It's our birthright to be celebrated for who we are. Practising gratitude for our differences is one of the quickest ways to transcend insecurity. It's the ultimate form of self-love. To be grateful for all that we are, and all that others are, is a mark of unconditional love. Often this means stepping outside our current frames of thinking or social norms to broaden our ideas of beauty.

GRATITUDE AND SUSTAINABILITY

I see gratitude as the way to make our creations sustainable. If you can learn something, create something, experience something and be in a state of gratitude, you help it become sustained, integrated, and consolidated. '

When someone breaks your heart, the prospect of being grateful for this experience seems a little difficult. However, to eventually land in gratitude for all experiences, we extract only the gifts. Practising gratitude is one of the ultimate demonstrations of self-love, shifting our focus onto that which enriches our lives. Gratitude is the safeguard that allows us to stay in love with life, and continue to love who we are, as we are, in this moment. To regret, resent or hate things from our past is to hold ourselves back from ever fully embracing who we are now.

As I mentioned earlier, rather than seeing time as the healer or the way to bring about peace, it's important to see that what time provides is actually perspective. Gratitude naturally provides a superior, more expansive perspective, and this is a powerful healer.

Gratitude is a practice.

For something to become a habit, the brain relies on repetitive action. It takes approximately twelve weeks to form any type of behavioural habit that strengthens neural pathways so that the brain will begin automatically commanding this behaviour. I highly recommend beginning a gratitude practice daily; at the same time, each day. Again, ritual is deeply embedded in who we are, and to become ritualistic in your practices will ensure the deep integration of the behaviours that lead a life of loving out loud.

MEDITATION AND PRAYER IS A TECHNOLOGY

Discovering that meditation and prayer as a technology radically transformed my thinking around practising awareness and gratitude. Meditation is a technology; the answer to your prayer is in the prayer. By asking for something, we automatically open ourselves to receiving. We move into openness. See this as a magnet for attracting what it is that you're wanting. To be in the vibration of what it is you're seeking is to become one with it. To practice gratitude for something you have yet to receive, is to vibrate at its frequency and become a magnet for it.

As discussed in Chapter 1, belief powers the existence of something. Without meditation, and conscious reframing we can often energise our problems. Meditation and prayer are a space to channel our belief into the desired outcome, rather than the worst-case scenarios. Some meditators call this process, "tapping into your unknown." Mediation gives space for what was unconscious to become conscious. It allows us to take a step back from the stimulation and distraction of the external world and become more aware of our internal world. It allows us to tap into the energy and the power of our unknown, and the more it is practised, the more you will vibrate in your wholeness.

It has been proven time and time again that when mass mediations have occurred, crime rates, deaths caused by war, and violence have been reported to decrease by up to 76%, in some cases, it was even documented that economic indicators improved. During the three largest peace-creating assemblies ever held in the West, statistics provided by the Rand Corporation showed a 72% reduction in worldwide terrorism.

For centuries, we have known that to pray and to meditate; to be focused on gratitude, forgiveness and joy, puts us into a state of transcendence. It is here we find the capacity to connect to source energy (love) and to find enhanced states of consciousness. But, the concept of practising gratitude has been watered-down, and we've lost our connection to the true abilities these practices have to improve our states of consciousness and give us a deeper sense of self-regulation and self-control. Meditation and prayer put us in the driver's seat of our own reality; we stop believing that the world happens to us and start to understand that we happen to the world.

Life happens because of us.

As I've mentioned, the brain responds and learns through repetition. It is because of this that through an ongoing practice you will find that over time your default position and perceptive will be one of a deeper connection to love and innerpeace. This is how, when my laptop hard drive was lost along with three years of work, and my new car was crashed before I had insured it, I had the immediate antifragility to respond with acceptance, love, and gratitude for the possibilities that could come out of these happenings. I understood that life is always working for me, regardless of how bad our perception of a situation may seem.

When we become aware of where we are failing to practice gratitude and forgiveness, there's an immense gift. Through the awareness of this, our practice becomes strengthened, as we are presented the opportunity to realign our hearts with our minds. One of the best ways to understand where we are failing to practice gratitude is to become aware of where we are experiencing resistance.

Take the time to journal the answers to these questions. Really reflect:

1. *Are there patterns in your life that you feel you're repeating over and over again?*

2. Do you experience the same type of toxicity in more than one of your relationships? (Now and in the past).

3. Where are you experiencing the most resistance in your life? What do you feel this is highlighting to you? What are you needing to become aware of?

4. What parts of your past do you continually revisit, finding it difficult to reconcile? What were the gifts in these experiences? What insights do you have today, because of their occurrence?

5. Are there people in your life you know to be extremely special and valuable to you, but rarely express that to?

6. What parts of yourself are you constantly critiquing, rather than appreciating?

CHAPTER 9: SERVICE

What is your quest?

Congratulations - you have reached the final chapter of your learning, and you're almost ready to begin fearlessly, and unapologetically, loving out loud.

Love is a bird's eye view, it's the ultimate perspective. To see things through the eyes of love is to have finally learnt what all those experiences had to teach us. It's to become complete with an experience. In Buddhism, it is taught that we have two factors to our experience; the actual experience we are having and the relationship we have to this experience. To be in a state of love is to be complete with all experiences; irrespective of what they are. It is difficult for a judging mind to understand this, and only through compassion can we learn the power of becoming one with our experiences.

When we begin to serve the world around us, rather than focusing on what it is we can gain, it is easier to be whole with our experiences. This is because we're not entering the experience with the mindset of what we can gain.

There's a way to speed up your process of learning; it's to understand the way love sees. Once you understand how love would see things, in their perfection, then you're more quickly about to guide yourself from your view back to love, and through love's perspective, gain a deeper understanding of the circumstance.

I distinctly recall being out to dinner in 2015, during my first term as a National Mental Health Commissioner, with extremely influential figures in the mental health space, the topic of human nature was raised. In passing, one of the psychiatrists said, "Well, human nature is innately selfish". I stopped him, seeking clarification as to whether or not I had heard him properly. The table, other than me, was in consensus that humans will innately act in self-interest as a fundamental condition of the human psychology. I felt an intense tightness in my chest. I had seen too many examples of human empathy, of giving freely. I became fascinated that this frame, and way of thinking, was the leading opinion, and began investigating it more deeply to find the truth.

Birthed from this insatiable curiosity, I began asking audience members in my talks, "Hands up how many people in the audience believe that human nature is innately selfish?" Always, almost all, hands are raised.

I want to bring a compelling counter-argument to this perceptive of selfishness by drawing upon two main bodies of research and philosophy.

1. Charles Darwin's theory of "Artificial Barriers."

2. The way human beings are biologically and neurologically wired for **connection.**

COMPASSION (LOVE) IS THE KEY TO OUR EVOLUTION

Charles Darwin is renowned for his most famous work The Theory of Evolution: Survival of the Fittest, written in 1864. Some of you may not have heard of some of Darwin's other theories, in particular, his Theory of Artificial Barriers, discussed in The Descent of Man. This theory explores how, as a species, we are one humanity, and our process of evolution will be the process of awakening to our oneness; breaking down what he called "artificial barriers." The barriers that separate us from each other, and extend our sympathies (which is the 1870's meant compassion), to all men unknown and known to him. Artificial Barriers mean things like nation states, race, education, social class, sexuality, and so on so forth.

"As man advances in civilization, and small tribes are united into larger communities, the simplest reason would tell each individual that he ought to extend his social instincts and sympathies to all members of the same nation, though personally unknown to him. This point being once reached, there is only an artificial barrier to prevent his sympathies extending to the men of all nations and races."

— Charles Darwin

These artificial barriers are influenced largely by nationalism; the idea that an act of brutality or prejudice done against someone from a different nation, or from part of a different community, is more justified and less inhumane than that done to someone from our own nation or community. It has created the separation of humanity, rather than unification. Yet it is our compassion to each other and to other species that has helped us evolve. It is a mark of our intelligence and expansion that we can see other animals with love and empathy, and that we can create systems of peaceful cohabitation, rather than brutality.

LOVE IS INGRAINED IN OUR BIOLOGY

All spiritual philosophies suggest that happiness, purpose, and fulfilment are found in service; in giving to others. And there are rational, practical explanations as to why this is true.

There are four hormones that keep us in a state of positive well-being that many of you may already know what they are;

Endorphins: assists us to mask pain - the reason runners experience a *'runner's high'*.

Dopamine: is released when we achieve something - *the feeling you get when you tick something off the to-do list or finish a project).*

Serotonin: is experienced when we feel a sense of pride, trust and love for our loved ones - *is designed to formulate strong social bonds with one another).*

Oxytocin: is experienced during physical touch - (*it's designed to create extreme bonds and feelings of closeness, e.g. mass amounts of oxytocin is released in a mother and child during birth to ensure an unbreakable bond).*

The interesting thing is that we are biologically and neurologically wired for connection. It feels good to make others feel good. When you break it down, it doesn't really seem like rocket science. Throughout our evolution we needed each other in order to survive, so would it not make sense that a part of our design would be one of cooperation, connection and sense of 'tribe' (or togetherness)? When you examine the way the brain is designed, serotonin and oxytocin are both entirely dependent on human connection. One of the rawest examples of this is when a mother gives birth to her baby, huge amounts of oxytocin flood both the mother and child in order to create a deep, unbreakable bond between the two. We experience oxytocin when we experience contact; human affection, intimacy, and a deep sense of love. When you have the sense of falling in love, oxytocin is responsible for creating this phenomenon (on a chemical level). Serotonin is in charge of feelings like trust and pride, crucial for a feeling of love and connection. It's even been studied that we experience a rush of serotonin when we watch an act of kindness that we aren't directly part of.

We are hardwired for connection. It's both a smart and crucial design in order for us to realise and cooperate in our interdependence.

WE BEGIN THE JOURNEY OF SELF-LOVE, IN ORDER TO ULTIMATELY LOVE OTHERS

Experiences will ultimately hold value because of their ability to bring us closer to connection. Experiences that connect us more deeply to ourselves, and thus each other, provide us with a deeper sense of fulfilment and meaning. As you've gone through each of these Chapters, each concept has brought you closer to a deep understanding of who you are. Once you begin realising your true nature, the joy of expressing yourself is found in giving to others.

WE CREATE, TO GIVE OURSELVES AWAY

The process of creation is the most beautifully designed process. To create is to enquire deep within yourself, to explore the deepest parts of your emotion, insights and nature, and then to draw it out of you and give it to others. It's a feeling of elation and the pathway of your highest joy. When you ask an actor what the experience is like receiving the final round of applause, or how an artist feels when they finally put their brush down, or the feeling a chef gets when they watch others enjoy their food - it is clear we are wired to offer what we possess to others. Greed, scarcity and fear stop us from understanding what is most natural to us.

To love each other is the most natural thing in the world.

To love is to know how easy this journey really can be. It is us expressing what we, ultimately, know to be true. We need each other and always have, for our wellbeing and survival. As a humanity, we are a family. When we can set down our differences and understand our sameness, we flourish.

During World War I, for the Christmas of 1914, it was suggested by Pope Benedict XV that soldiers call a Christmas truce. Never in history had this been seen. Soldiers from both sides climbed across the trenches, unarmed, to wish their enemies a Merry Christmas. The soldiers sang Christmas Carols and shared gifts of cigarettes and plum pudding. For 24 hours, the war had ceased and the seemingly irreconcilable differences were put to rest. This story has, for over a century, been offered as a phenomenal story of goodwill. It demonstrated our natural state as a species; when we have permission to connect, and to love we will choose it.

To follow our hearts is not an airy-fairy, illusive, feel good 'idea'. It is the strongest direction we can travel. It's the compass that will always lead us to truth; to sovereignty, to joy. Our hearts have an intelligence our minds will never be able to fully understand. Man has forever looked to religion, to the skies, and to philosophy to find meaning and guidance. We know on a very deep level that love is our end game. We go through these experiences of hate, greed, jealousy, dishonesty, misdirection, lust, all to ultimately know that we are love.

All roads lead to love.

Because our hearts know this, and ultimately we will all awaken to this, we can stay connected to our nature by always remaining in service to one another. This might be by answering our friend's phone call in a crisis, or to helping our struggling co-worker, or even to having compassion for another's ignorance. To do this is to also be in service ourselves. It's the greatest form of expression we have; to love each other.

WE MEET OURSELVES THROUGH EACH OTHER

The ultimate light bulb moment for me was realising how self-focused and self-absorbed my mindset was during the darkest times in my life. Separating from my darkness meant shifting my focus from myself to what I could offer to others. This provided the ultimate meaning for me and has single-handedly been the catalyst in my journey to Love Out Loud. I never underestimate how blessed I am to work with the people I've worked with. I'm convinced beyond any measure that we are all deeply connected, interwoven and interdependent. As humanity, we have such a shiveringly beautiful opportunity to awaken to our oneness. My breath is taken away when I think about the possibilities we are given in this life to truly understand what we are. The ways we can choose to step out of insecurities (in-security) and surrender the need to protect ourselves, so that we may choose love instead.

For so long I believed I was the crazy one for seeing the truth, for thinking a different way and seeing beyond the masks and the superficiality. I hurt myself for my difference and my sensitivity before I realised the power in harnessing my humanity. Just as there's incredible power in harnessing yours. There's a power in your sensitivity that no words can describe or capture. Within your sensitivity and your compassion, is your roadmap back to love, and back to truth.

REFLECTING ON YOUR JOURNEY

The process you've undergone is not to be underestimated. You've ventured through nine chapters, and three major components of your transformation; from separating yourself from your comfort zone to undertaking a challenge, to finally now, reintegrating and acknowledging this new version of yourself. You've asked yourself many confrontational questions and dove into parts of yourself, and your philosophy, that has likely forever changed you.

I saw one of my favourite speakers during 2017, and he said, "When you place a certain amount of consciousness over your life, there is no going back." It has stuck with me because I know it to be true. Ultimately, knowledge is power, reflection is learning, and enquiry creates permanent and real transformation. I have such deep appreciation and gratitude for playing a role in your journey. It has been an honour to share ten years of wisdom in a single book with you. I trust you bring this with you to your service to humanity.

It's important that you take the time to properly reflect on the process you've been through, and for this reason, I have written out a synopsis of everything we have covered.

Chapter one: Belief: What are you searching for?

Key Concepts	Key Reflection Questions
1. Principles of Love. - Love is not found in another, it is a self-perpetuated experience. - Love is your NATURE. - Becoming complete with love is a process of aligning your heart and mind. - Life is not happening to you, you are happening to life; the outside world is a mirror of your internal world; to reach a state of self-love is to see love (you) in all things. - Evolution is happening, regardless of whether or not we are consciously participating in it. 2. Belief systems are your filters. 3. Belief systems are changeable. 4. We must learn the functionality of the brain, to beat it. 5. Perspective heals us, not time.	1. What are the reasons you're feeling disconnected? 2. What are the biggest pain points in your life? 3. What are you wanting to align yourself with? Otherwise asked; how are you wanting to feel? (For example; free, successful, expansive, joyous, grateful). 4. What are the negative belief systems you hold about yourself? 5. Where could you evolve your perception?

Chapter 2: Honesty: What do you truly want?

Key Concepts	Key Reflection Questions
1. Necessities over niceties. 2. Truth is a state of being, honesty is the practice. 3. It's okay to say, "No." 4. The Nature of Truth. 5. Shame and Fear blocking your expression of truth. 6. Conscious Communication. 7. Blame vs. Need.	1. What do you really want? 2. What do you truly desire? 3. What is stopping you from being in and speaking your truth? 4. What do you want, need, and feel? 5. Where are you blaming others, or life, for your misfortunes? 6. What areas of life are you needing to take responsibility?

Chapter 3: Acceptance: What terrifies you about letting go of who you think you are?

Key Concepts	Key Reflection Questions
1. Get really good at failing.	1. What is your current identity, and does it fulfil you?
2. Accepting your truth is crucial in order to progress in your journey.	2. What is your current relationship with failure?
	3. How do you currently define success?
3. You must accept yourself, before anyone else can.	4. Where are you looking for approval or validation?
	5. Where have you drawn conclusions that haven't served you?
4. Do not wait for permission to follow your dreams.	6. Where are your judgements ruling you and blocking you from truth/love?
5. Overcome your biases and choose love.	
6. Fear is reactive, love is responsive.	

Chapter 4: Death: What are you willing to die for?

Key Concepts	Key Reflection Questions
1. We experience many figurative deaths in our life. 2. We can consciously choose how our rebirth looks. 3. To be fully alive, and to live with meaning, we must realise our mortality. 4. We live in relationship to all things. 5. Relationships are mirrors for our own evolution. 6. Love is freedom, fear is control. 7. Pain assists us to learn presence. 8. Overcome judgment.	1. What are you attached to? 2. What do you need to let go of? 3. How would you live your life differently if you knew you were going to die tomorrow? 4. What have the gifts in your pain been? 5. What triggers you and what does this show you?

Chapter 5: Purpose: How does love rise up in you?

Key Concepts	Key Reflection Questions
1. Purpose is not what you do, but rather who you are being. 2. Purpose is responsive and flexible. 3. Struggle pushes us towards purpose. 4. Purpose deepens your capacity to love. 5. Discovering purpose requires space. 6. You can tell you're on purpose when you love who you're being. 7. Identifying purpose is about analysing loves emotional, physical and psychological effects on you.	1. What do you stand for? 2. Who do you want to be? 3. How does love rise up in you emotionally? 4. How do you think when you're in love? 5. What do you feel in your body when you're in love? 6. What is your capacity to love? 7. What is the value you bring to the world?

Chapter 6: Creativity: How will you birth your purpose into the world?

Key Concepts	Key Reflection Questions
1. You are fundamentally creative. 2. Creativity requires the ability to quantify. 3. Failure stimulates creativity. 4. Love has always got your back. 5. Judgment is a killer of creativity; curiosity allows creativity to flourish. 6. Ask the right questions. 7. Let appreciation lead to inspired action.	1. What are some of the things you're wanting to create in your life at the moment? 2. What questions are you asking in life? 3. What are the judgments and conditions around what you're wanting to create for yourself? 4. What inspires you? 5. Where can you shift destructive behaviour into constructive behaviour? 6. How do you generally frame things in life?

Chapter 7: Acknowledgement: How can you alchemise your pain into beauty?

Key Concepts	Key Reflection Questions
1. Acknowledgement assists you in turning pain into diamonds. 2. Acknowledgement is confrontational; that's why it's powerful and transformative. 3. Your life unfolds in proportion to your courage. 4. When you aren't accustomed to receiving acknowledgment, you may initially become defensive. 5. To take responsibility for your life, you must acknowledge your past. 6. Acknowledgement generates connection. 7. Ritual is crucial.	1. What are you not acknowledging in your life or your past? 2. What do you avoid or deflect? 3. How easy is it for you to receive love and acknowledgement? 4. Where is fear trumping your expression of courage? 5. Where have you avoided taking responsibility for yourself? 6. What are your rituals? 7. Where is the distinction between what's sacred and mundane in your life?

Chapter 8: Gratitude: How can love become your ultimate perspective?

Key Concepts	Key Reflection Questions
1. Fear and anger cannot exist in the same space as gratitude. 2. Gratitude is the state of receiving. 3. Gratitude allows us to sustain and grow the gift in our lives. 4. Gratitude allows us to bring light to our darkness. 5. Integrity is to love those who hate you. 6. Gratitude is the bridge to motivation. 7. Meditation is a technology.	1. What are the patterns you're repeating over and over again? 2. What is still unresolved in your past? 3. What is your gratitude practice? 4. What have been the gifts, and lessons, in some of your hardest times? 5. What are the areas of your life you are always criticizing, and how can you bring more appreciation to them?

Chapter 9: Service: What is your quest?

Key Concepts	Key Reflection Questions
1. Humans are wired for connection. 2. Compassion and empathy is crucial for our evolution. 3. Love is ingrained in our biology. 4. We begin the journey of self-love to ultimately love others. 5. We create, to give ourselves away. 6. We meet ourselves through each other.	1. What is your quest? 2. How do you wish to serve humanity? 3. What legacy do you want to leave in this world? 4. How committed are you to Loving Out Loud? 5. How do you want to express your love, moving forward?

There are many questions here for you to always come back to in order to refocus and recentre yourself.

Take your time to really go deep before you close the final page in this book.

If you're still wanting to go deeper and expand on all of these concepts, Love OUT LOUD has an online course which you can find via *www.nicolegibson. com.au*.

There is a whole community of us around the world who are ready to truly begin the revolution of love.

You are loved. I love you, and I trust that at this point of the journey, you genuinely feel and know that.

I don't need to know you, or even to have met you, to know that I love you. My mission here is to remember the deepest part of our humanity. It's in this place where we meet that there is no distance, no separation, no judgment, no hate, no segregation.

As a teenager, I felt lonely. I felt so far away from the people I connected with, people like Bob Marley, John Lennon and Nelson Mandela. The older I got, the more I understood there was no distance between me and them. Love is the ultimate unifier. Love knows no bounds. I would read some of my hero's quotes, like these:

Bob Marley;

"I don't believe in death, neither in flesh nor in spirit."

"Don't gain the world and lose your soul. Wisdom is better than silver and gold."

"Put your vision to reality."

"Every man gotta right to decide his own destiny."

John Lennon

"You may say I'm a dreamer, but I'm not the only one. I hope someday you'll join us, and the world will live as one."

"A dream you dream alone is only a dream. A dream you dream together is reality."

"I believe in God, but not as one thing, not as an old man in the sky. I believe that what people call God is something in all of us. I believe that what Jesus and Mohammed and Buddha and all the rest said was right. It's just that the translations have gone wrong."

"If someone thinks that peace and love are just a cliché that must have been left behind in the 60s, that's a problem. Peace and love are eternal."

"Limitless undying love which shines around me like a million suns it calls me on and on across the universe."

"Love is a promise, love is a souvenir, once given never forgotten, never let it disappear."

Nelson Mandela

"It always seems impossible until it's done."

"For to be free is not merely to cast off one's chains, but to live in a way that respects and enhances the freedom of others."

"I learned that courage was not the absence of fear, but the triumph over it. The brave man is not he who does not feel afraid, but he who conquers that fear."

"And as we let our own light shine, we unconsciously give other people permission to do the same" (as he quoted Marianne Williamson)

"There is no passion to be found playing small - in settling for a life that is less than the one you are capable of living."

It was these people that paved the way back to light. I am merely here to be the one that holds the torch for you, as you walk back to your truth.

Love is free. We stand on the shoulders of giants. Truly, we do. *Be humble.* We are servants to a much greater plan, a much greater fabric. You are unrepeatable and irreplaceable. Your worth can never be compromised.

You do not need to search for love, you are already it.

End the war in your own mind, and go forth in your totality; the understanding that your potential is limitless, that the fear you experience is never a match to the truth in your heart.

To be in service to love, to be the uplifter, the supporter, the lover, is the ultimate path to awakening.

I want you to live in love, I want you to transcend the prison I watch so many people create for themselves. I want you to listen and hear the words of the greatest prophets that have walked the earth, and truly know your nature. Know thyself. Stop playing small and sacrificing this precious life we have been gifted. This isn't forever, you are going to die. It's guaranteed. So, what are you waiting for? Now is the time. It's your turn to Love OUT LOUD, it's your turn to turn your back on mediocrity, social pressure, parental expectations, fear, and walk the path less travelled, make something beautiful from the pain of your past and begin living your destiny.

Travel well, brother or sister. Your journey is only just beginning.